What Every Teacher
Should Know About

Student Assessment

What Every Teacher Should Know About ...

What Every Teacher Should Know About
Diverse Learners

What Every Teacher Should Know About
Student Motivation

What Every Teacher Should Know About
Learning, Memory, and the Brain

What Every Teacher Should Know About
Instructional Planning

What Every Teacher Should Know About
Effective Teaching Strategies

What Every Teacher Should Know About
Classroom Management and Discipline

What Every Teacher Should Know About
Student Assessment

What Every Teacher Should Know About
Special Learners

What Every Teacher Should Know About
Media and Technology

What Every Teacher Should Know About
The Profession and Politics of Teaching

DONNA WALKER TILESTON

What Every Teacher Should Know About
Student Assessment

CORWIN PRESS
A Sage Publications Company
Thousand Oaks, California

For information:

Corwin Press
A Sage Publications Company
2455 Teller Road
Thousand Oaks, California 91320
www.corwinpress.com

Sage Publications Ltd.
6 Bonhill Street
London EC2A 4PU
United Kingdom

Sage Publications India Pvt. Ltd.
B-42, Panchsheel Enclave
Post Box 4109
New Delhi 110 017   India

Printed in the United States of America

Library of Congress Cataloging-in-Publication Data

Tileston, Donna Walker.
What every teacher should know about student assessment /
Donna Walker Tileston.
        p. cm. — (What every teacher should know about—; 7)
Includes bibliographical references and index.
ISBN 0-7619-3123-6 (pbk.)
    1. Educational tests and measurements. 2. Examinations. I. Title II. Series:
Tileston, Donna Walker. What every teacher should know about—7.
LB3051.T564 2004
371.26—dc21   2003010240

This book is printed on acid-free paper.

03   04   05   06   10   9   8   7   6   5   4   3   2   1

Acquisitions Editor:	Faye Zucker
Editorial Assistant:	Stacy Wagner
Production Editor:	Diane S. Foster
Copy Editor:	Stacey Shimizu
Typesetter:	C&M Digitals (P) Ltd.
Proofreader:	Mary Meagher
Indexer:	Molly Hall
Cover Designer:	Tracy E. Miller
Graphic Designer:	Lisa Miller

Contents

1408

107447

About the Author

Donna Walker Tileston, Ed.D., is a veteran teacher of 27 years and the president of Strategic Teaching and Learning, a consulting firm that provides services to schools throughout the United States and Canada. Also an author, Donna's publications include *Strategies for Teaching Differently: On the Block or Not* (Corwin Press, 1998), *Innovative Strategies of the Block Schedule* (Bureau of Education and Research [BER], 1999), and *Ten Best Teaching Practices: How Brain Research, Learning Styles, and Standards Define Teaching Competencies* (Corwin Press, 2000), which has been on Corwin's best-seller list since its first year in print.

Donna received her B.A. from the University of North Texas, her M.A. from East Texas State University, and her Ed.D. from Texas A & M University-Commerce. She may be reached at www.strategicteaching&learning.com or by e-mail at dwtileston@yahoo.com.

Acknowledgments

M y sincere thanks go to my Acquisitions Editor, Faye Zucker, for her faith in education and what this information can do to help all children be successful. Without Faye, these books would not have been possible.

I had the best team of editors around: Diane Foster, Stacy Wagner, and Stacey Shimizu. You took my words and you gave them power. Thank you.

Thanks to my wonderful Board Chairman at Strategic Teaching and Learning, Dulany Howland: Thank you for sticking with me in the good times and the tough spots. Your expertise and friendship have been invaluable.

To my wonderful parents, Jack and Jacqueline Walker.

Introduction

We live in a time when government, business and industry, and the general public are calling for an accounting of student abilities. Because single-test instruments are more easily available for assessment, they are the assessment of choice. As teachers, we know that a single assessment in a written, forced-choice format is not the best way to determine student success. We know there are better choices for us. While we have little control over the state-mandated test measures, we do have tremendous control over the day-to-day measures that we use in our classrooms.

This book will examine current research on performance (i.e., *authentic*) assessment, appropriate teacher-made tests, and standardized tests. Standards-based instruction will be discussed along with its the implications for the classroom. The effectiveness of seven kinds of student achievement tests will be explored. Information on assessment, monitoring instructional effectiveness, and the implications for the classroom will be included. We will examine standardized tests, teacher-made tests, multiple and authentic assessments, portfolios, and self-assessments. How to prepare a rubric will be discussed, and we will walk through a classroom unit, planning with the end in mind by selecting objectives (formative, summative, procedural, and declarative), preparing a rubric, identifying the assessment tools to be used, and evaluating the effectiveness of the assessment.

Marzano (1998) found that teaching vocabulary to students first has a high impact on achievement. With that in mind, I have provided a list of vocabulary words that will be a part of this book. Using Form 0.1, see how many of the words you recognize. Write your definition in the space provided, and then review your answers as you read. By the way, this is an effective way to teach vocabulary to your students.

In addition, I am providing a vocabulary pre-test for you based on the information from this book. After you have read the book, you will be given a post-test and the solutions to the tests. The Vocabulary Summary offers additional information about these and other terms associated with motivation.

Form 0.1   Vocabulary List for Assessment

Vocabulary Word	Your Definition	Your Revised Definition
Achievement gap		
Accountability		
Alignment		
Aptitude tests		
Assessment		
At-risk students		
Authentic assessment		
Benchmark		
Competency tests		
Criterion-referenced tests		
Data-based decision making		
Disaggregated data		
Formal assessment		
Formative assessment		
High-stakes testing *Intelligence testing*		

Form 0.1   Continued

Measures of central tendency		
Natural distribution		
Norm-referenced tests		
Peer assessment		
Performance tasks		
Portfolio		
Reliability		
Rubric		
Self-assessment		
Standardized tests		
Standards		
Student understanding		
Summative assessment		
Validity		

Vocabulary Pre-Test

Instructions: Choose the one best answer for the questions provided.

1. Mr. Conner wants to know if his students can apply the information they learned on estimation. Which assessment would be the best way to determine whether the students can apply what they know?
   A. Multiple-choice test
   B. Forced-choice text
   C. Self-assessment
   D. Performance task

2. A test that determines whether a student graduates from high school is . . .
   A. Criterion referenced
   B. High stakes
   C. Norm referenced
   D. A performance task

3. In a normal distribution, what percentage of the scores falls within two standard deviations of the mean?
   A. 95%
   B. 90%
   C. 85%
   D. 97%

4. The XYZ Testing Company is retesting a group of students to see how closely the test scores match the first test given. For what are they testing?
   A. Validity
   B. Performance
   C. Reliability
   D. Bias

5. Using measures of central tendency, when would it be appropriate to use the mode?
   A. When the standard deviation is zero.
   B. When the scores are average.
   C. When a large number of the scores are the same.
   D. When there is a large distribution in the scores.

6. Which term reflects the spread of scores around the mean?
   A. Standard deviation
   B. Median
   C. Mode
   D. Validity

7. A test given to determine what students have learned in order to plan instruction is . . .
   A. A norm-referenced test
   B. Formative assessment
   C. A forced-choice test
   D. An aptitude test

8. A test given to document what a student has learned is called . . .
   A. Summative assessment
   B. An aptitude test
   C. A criterion-referenced test
   D. Formative assessment

9. Martin School makes a strong effort to ensure that what is written in their curriculum documents is what is taught in the classroom and what is tested. This practice is know as . . .

A. Competency
B. Data-based decision making
C. Benchmarks
D. Alignment

10. Martin School regularly looks at test scores to determine if male students are performing as well as female students and to see that minorities are making the same level of progress as majority students. This practice is called . . .
A. Prevention of bias
B. Disaggregating data
C. Setting benchmarks
D. Authentic assessment

11. The teachers at Martin School have taken the information from test scores, as well as attendance and dropout rates, to use in planning for student needs. This practice is called . . .
A. Benchmarking
B. Disaggregating data
C. Data-based decision making
D. Using reliability

12. Martin School is examining student test scores, particularly to compare male and female scores and the scores of students by race. For what are they most likely looking?
A. Validity
B. Achievement gaps
C. Reliability
D. Norms

13. To measure students' progress over time on performance tasks, which type of assessment would most likely be used?
A. Portfolios
B. Forced-choice tests
C. Achievement tests
D. Norm-referenced tests

14. To test declarative knowledge, a teacher would probably use which type of assessment?
    A. Forced-choice tests
    B. Portfolios
    C. Performance tasks
    D. Observation

15. To test procedural knowledge, a teacher would probably use which type of assessment?
    A. Multiple-choice tests
    B. Essay
    C. True/false tests
    D. Observation

16. Mr. Conner's school resides in a state that has adopted state curriculum standards for which students are tested annually. This practice is often referred to as . . .
    A. Assessment
    B. Authentic assessment
    C. Alignment
    D. Accountability

17. On the XYZ test, about 20% of the students failed, about 20% did very well, and the rest of the students scored in between. This is called . . .
    A. Reliability
    B. Validity
    C. Normal distribution
    D. Standardization

18. The measure that is applied to learning is called . . .
    A. Reliability
    B. Assessment
    C. Evaluation
    D. Validity

19. Which type of test most closely assesses how well students know state standards?
    A. Criterion-referenced tests
    B. Aptitude tests

   C. Formative assessments
   D. Norm-referenced tests

20. Which of the following is *not* true of state testing?
   A. They are formative in nature.
   B. They are summative in nature.
   C. They are based on content standards.
   D. They are based on performance standards.

Making Decisions About Assessment

The standard dictionary definition of learning is simple. Learning is related to knowledge and understanding. Yet, many of the world's top neuroscientists would have a tough time defining how to measure learning. Why? Much of what is important learning cannot be measured at this time. Examples of the hard to measure include our so-called mental models of how things work, critical neuronal connections, our values, our capability beliefs, the degree of personal transference and depth of meaning.

—Eric Jensen, *Completing the Puzzle*

Assessment is a fact of life, whether we like it or not. We are all being assessed daily according to the decisions we make and the way that we carry out those decisions. Our students are being held accountable to the public for declarative and procedural information through a myriad of tests designed to show competency and used at the state and national level for comparison of schools.

Much of the controversy regarding testing is due to the fact that most assessment measures used for state and national standards rely heavily on declarative information (e.g., facts, formulas, places, people, and names) rather than procedural information (e.g., the ability to use declarative information). Many educators argue that testing primarily declarative information does not give a true picture of how well students understand the learning. Procedural knowledge, however, is difficult to measure on standardized tests and, although test makers have made significant progress in the last few years, most standardized tests do not truly measure the depth of knowledge required for real-world application.

EXAMINING DECLARATIVE AND PROCEDURAL INFORMATION

Declarative information is the factual information that is a part of every subject's curriculum. Declarative information is what students know in terms of facts, dates, names, concepts, and so forth. An example of a declarative objective for a lesson might be, "Students will know the steps necessary to check subtraction." Note that at the declarative level, students can repeat the steps on paper or orally; it does not mean they can perform the steps. Being able to use the information in some way comes under the classification of procedural objectives. For example, a procedural objective might say, "Students will execute the steps necessary to check subtraction in a given problem."

I make this distinction because what we test most at this time is the declarative rather than the procedural. Just being able to write the steps does not mean that the student understands them or that he can use them. As Jensen (1997) said, we still do not know if the student has a mental model of how to execute the information. For that matter, we do not know that the student even understands the factual information he or she has learned. This is an important distinction as we look at meaningful assessment. What do we really want to know as a result of the assessment? Do we want to know that our students know the steps, or do we want to know that they can use those steps in a meaningful way—or both?

Designing Assessments

One of the dilemmas that we face as teachers is how to design an assessment that will tell us our students' level of understanding. So many times, classroom assessments that depend solely on paper and pen measure only show surface understanding of the principles involved in the learning. How, then, can we build assessment instruments that effectively measure student learning?

When designing assessment for the classroom, there is a series of questions that needs to be answered.

What is important for students to know and be able to do? This question is not just about assessing knowledge at a given grade level or in a subject sequence, but goes beyond to ask what students need to know and be able to do *in life.* Wiggins and McTighe (1998) say that learning should have "enduring value beyond the classroom." What do they mean? Assessment should do more than determine facts, dates, times, and formulas. Assessment should provide information about what the students know and whether they can apply that information in a real-world context

Is the knowledge or process critical to the discipline? Teaching the genres of literature goes to the heart of the subject matter and would be important to assess in terms of declarative knowledge (being able to identify various genres and their characteristics) and procedural knowledge (being able to write in various genres). At this early stage of developing assessment instruments, it is important to use both declarative and procedural formats. Having students just repeat information learned is not enough; we must ask how students can use the information to make them better citizens, better readers, more effective leaders, more productive, and successful adults.

How will we know that students understand the learning? We have all had the experience of reading a page from a book and then at the end wondering what in the world we read. Minds wander, and we may go through the motions without really knowing what we read or listened to or talked about. As a teacher, it is important to design assessments that get at the heart of the learning. What misconceptions might students have? What are the underlying principles or concepts that might be missed? Is there evidence that the items being assessed have been taught (not just introduced) in the classroom? Do the items being assessed relate back to curriculum that has been deemed to be important for students to know and understand? Are there written declarative and procedural objectives that relate directly to the items being assessed?

In trying to gauge whether students understand the learning, we need to consider reliability and validity. Reliability and validity are critical to effective assessment, whether the assessment is at the classroom, district, state, or national level. If a test does not truly measure what we intend for students to know and be able to do, it has no validity. We have just gone through the motions. Where there is no validity, we tend to just teach to the test. Reliability goes to the source of the information. Is the test tied to the curriculum, or to local, state, and national standards? Will the information and processes necessary for success on the assessment be taught sufficiently so that students will be able to apply them to any test on the subject? We want to move away from the "gotchas" where students are tested on information they have not learned.

Is the assessment in alignment with the written and taught curriculum? Figure 1.1 shows how assessment should be aligned with our written and taught curriculum. We often see the model presented in Figure 1.1, but we may not have considered the implications, whether it is the teacher, the curriculum department, or the state.

Let's look at a sample test question and analyze it from the standpoint of the previous questions raised about creating

Figure 1.1   The Aligned Curriculum

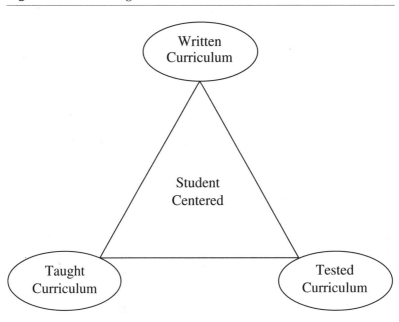

good assessments. Suppose that a question over *The Great Gatsby* on a given assessment asks, "Was Nick a true friend to Gatsby? Give reasons for your answer." On the surface, this is a great question, because it asks the student to read between the lines of the story, to make inferences, to put information into perspective, and to be able to explain his or her answers. However, some questions must be answered to determine if the question is appropriate. Can this question be traced back to written objectives in the curriculum that require the learner to make inferences, to be able to interpret, or to see perspective? Were students made aware of the objectives and how was this done? Were objectives given to the students in written form, or were they put up in the room so that students could see the expectations? Were the objectives a part of the rubric for the learning? Were students taught how to make inferences, to interpret, or to see perspective? If the answer to any of these questions is "no," then the assessment is not aligned with the written and taught curriculum. When we assess students on tactics or information that is not a part of the written or taught curriculum, we refer to the test question as a "gotcha." Good assessments get rid of the "gotchas" by being aligned with the written objectives and the taught objectives for the learning.

I never give my students an assessment over anything for which they have not been given a rubric or a matrix that tells them exactly what the expectation is for the learning. I worked in a school that completely turned around the achievement level of its students, moving from being on the state's endangered list for low test scores to absolutely knocking the top off of the state test. One of the things that we did that made the most difference in student success was to give students a matrix that told them what we expected—and we gave it to them in advance. We will discuss this more in Chapter 3 as we look at how to build a matrix or rubric.

BUILDING BRAIN-COMPATIBLE ASSESSMENTS

We cannot fully take away test anxiety, nor can we remove nervousness about being assessed, even informally. We can, however, lessen the anxiety. We do this first by being sure that the written, taught, and tested curriculum is in alignment. By doing that, we get away from the "gotchas" and come closer to really assessing what is important for our students to know and be able to do.

Second, we can lessen the anxiety by providing adequate time for students to learn and by using both massed practice (i.e., practice provided in a concise amount of time) and practice that takes place over a longer period of time. For example, as a teacher, I might introduce a concept and work with my students on that concept for three days as massed practice. I know that they are more likely to remember and use the learning, however, if I return to the concept over time.

Third, we can help our students by providing adequate time and support as they learn the skills necessary to use the learning. We need to provide opportunities for students to practice the learning in the presence of the teacher before moving them to independent practice—especially independent practice for which they will be assessed, as in the case of homework. In the studies conducted at Mid-continent Regional Educational Laboratory (McREL; Marzano, 1998), the effect on student learning was very high when students were given opportunities to practice the learning with specific feedback from the teacher.

Practice is only effective if students are given adequate and frequent feedback so that they know when they have perfected a tactic or algorithm necessary to carry out the procedural objective. Feedback is not simply saying, "Good job." Feedback is specific, and it is both diagnostic and prescriptive. Tell students what they are doing right and what needs work, and make suggestions for how to make changes in the process. Marzano (1998) found that providing specific feedback to students at this stage of the learning has a profound effect on student learning. It can literally take a student from failure to success.

Guidelines

Based on Jensen's (1997) seven keys to helping us as we build brain-compatible assessments, the following questions are offered as a guide.

Are there observable behavior changes as a result of the learning? Students who are actively involved in the learning show it. They get excited, they are focused, and they tend to work in their preferred modality (auditory, visual, or kinesthetic) when given choices in the way that they are assessed. For example, when I give my adult learners a math question, I offer them choices for solving it based on their preferred way to learn. I tell the visual learners that they can draw the answer, the kinesthetic learners that they can act out the solution, and the auditory learners that they can work on the formula. I understand that this does not work well on a long assessment, but for day-to-day assessments, it is interesting to watch how students work out the answer. By observing my students in action, I am able to determine the learning and assessment preferences of my students, which helps me as a teacher to make the learning more meaningful. An added bonus is that when I give students choices, more students demonstrate understanding.

Are we making a difference in the students' biases toward the learning? I like to give my students a pre- and post-test on the subject matter that I am teaching—not on the factual subject matter but on their attitude toward it. Sometimes called *climate surveys,* such tests are great tools for discovering the hidden biases or fears of my students toward the upcoming learning, and they help me as I assure them that they can and will learn. A student's sense of self-efficacy—the belief by the student that he or she can learn, because he or she has had past success with the learning—is one of the most important aspects in getting and keeping our students' attention. Self-efficacy is different from self-esteem, because self-efficacy is based on fact, not just hope. Based on my climate survey, I can determine which students need help in building self-efficacy toward the subject matter. Students who have positive experiences with the assessment will have greater self-efficacy toward the subject.

Do students exhibit rational thinking? People who have rational thinking toward a subject are more likely to be able to transfer information learned in one subject to another. They will also be able to see the big picture of how the information fits into real-world activities. Good teaching and testing will lead students to have better rational-thinking abilities.

What is the quality of the mental models? According to Jensen (1998), "A mental model is a way of thinking about something. It is also a set of organizing principles which describe how something works (a democracy works best when we all participate). . . . In school, the best way to build mental models is through drawings, interviews, graphic organizers, projects, demonstrations, speeches, and role-plays." Students who understand the taught curriculum should be able to demonstrate on assessments that they have a clear mental model of the declarative and procedural objectives involved.

Do students exhibit personal relevance and integration? Students who truly understand should be able to apply the learning to themselves either through empathy, examples, relating the learning, or real-world examples. We should directly teach students how the learning is personal to them. Marzano (1998) found that when we make connections between the new learning and what students already know, we make a tremendous difference in the students' learning.

What are the strategies and skills that students know? Strategies and skills relate to the procedural knowledge that our students demonstrate. These strategies should be so embedded that they become second nature (i.e., students should be able to perform them without much conscious thought). For example, students who know the multiplication tables can perform multiplication strategies without a great deal of effort; students who know how to use a Bunsen burner can do so without deep concentration; and students who know how to speak a second language can answer questions in that language effortlessly.

How do we identify whether students have mastered the content? Students who have truly mastered the curriculum know what they know and how they learned it. Jensen (1997) says,

> Rote math and trivia facts alone are of little value. Instead, assess your students' grasp of the big picture. For example, in mathematics, can your students take a concept like lines and demonstrate where and how they are expressed mathematically? Help your learners to see how lines are important in their lives.

ALIGNMENT AND STANDARDS

The following exercise may be helpful as you look at your own state standards in light of alignment with what you are teaching and testing. Go to your state education Website and locate information about your state test. Most state education departments can be found by using this format: www.[state's first letter followed by *ea* or *de*].state.[state abbreviation].us. For example, the Texas education Website is www.tea.state.tx.us and the Oregon site is www.ode.state.or.us. Not every state follows this pattern, but you can also find your state by using a search engine like Google (www.google.com) and typing in the name of your state plus the phrase *Department of Education*.

Once you have found the Website, locate the information about the test for your grade level and/or subject area, or the test that most suits your grade level. If you teach in an area that is not directly tested, choose reading standards for the grade level closest to the one you teach. Next, choose three objectives that will be covered on the state test. You have learned that all assessment should be aligned with written and taught curriculum: Can you align the three objectives that you have chosen to the written curriculum for the state or for your school? When and how is this information taught to students?

In summary, we cannot test or assess everything we teach, so it is important to decide what it is important to assess. What do students need to know and be able to do through this body of information?

Most researchers in the field of assessment call for a backward design of instruction; in other words, they suggest teachers begin with the end in mind. When planning lessons, start with the assessment. What kinds of things will you want to assess as a result of the lessons? What do you want your students to be able to demonstrate to you as a result of the learning? What do you want them to know? From that information and from the state objectives, build declarative and procedural objectives for the learning. Next, provide a matrix or rubric that tells students exactly what your expectation is for them in terms of the objectives. As a last step, check the objectives, the lesson activities, and the assessment instrument to see if they are aligned. If not, then the assessment is a "gotcha."

2

Identifying and Enhancing Student Understanding

Let's make what's important more measurable instead of what's measurable, more important.

* * *

Immediate, tangible, measurable results are often expected in learning, even though the best learning takes time.

—Eric Jensen, *Completing the Puzzle*

One of the most difficult tasks that we have been assigned as teachers is assessing student learning. How do we truly know when our students have sufficient knowledge, understanding, and the skills required to be successful with the learning? In short, how do we know that our students know?

Traditional Ideas on
Checking for Understanding

One only has to bring up standardized testing in a group meeting of teachers to start a controversial and often heated discussion. Every state now has a standardized test on which students must demonstrate adequate understanding in order to advance at some point in their school years. The advancement may be from one grade to another, at grade intervals, or for graduation. Although the tests are a single measure, they may be taken more than once if they are not mastered the first time. Testing companies and statisticians have long used various methods to determine students' ability and understanding. We are all familiar with the bell curve that represents the fact that, generally, all scores fall within two standard deviations of the mean—thus, the cluster around the middle of the bell shape. Measures of central tendency are used to determine the "average student."

Let's look at a set of scores on a given exam for twenty students in the same classroom (see Table 2.1).

By adding up all of the scores and dividing by 20 (the number of students who took the test), we are able to determine that the mean score was 73.5. Usually, we use the mean score to determine what is generally called the class average. However, in the scores in our fictitious school, there are several very high scores and some very low scores. For sets of scores where there are clusters of very high or very low scores, the median, rather than the mean, is often used as the average. To get the median for this set of scores, it is necessary to list the scores from highest to lowest and then identify the middle score. In this case, the median score is 80.5. Mode is the score in a distribution that appears most frequently. In our group of scores, the mode is 85.

A more appropriate measure in terms of brain research might be to look at each student individually to determine if they are making adequate progress. Where they are not, additional measures need to be taken into account and other options for assistance for the student. I remember a particular

Table 2.1   Student Scores

Angelo, M.	85	Martinez, R.	62
Appleby, K.	35	Massey, J.	44
Betts, L.	99	Natori, S.	68
Blake, U.	97	Neal, P.	85
Cho, T.	92	Openheimer, L.	85
Drake, M.	97	Percy, M.	60
Edgar, K.	38	Robbins, C.	85
Franks, P.	77	Timmons, M.	81
Klinger, C.	85	Watson, S.	54
Lord, E.	66	Wilson, P.	80

Note: Scores arranged from highest to lowest.

Mean score is 73.5

Median score (the midpoint in the scores) = 80.5

Mode score (the score most often given) = 85

first-grade student I had who could not read. His mother had talked with doctors, special education personnel, and a psychologist to try to determine why the young man could not read. Some of the advice that the parent received was that the child was lazy and did not want to read. I have been in education many, many years, and I have never known a first-grader who did not read simply because he or she was lazy.

When we did visual testing on the first-graders, I noticed that this young man could not name any letter that was curved. I got some cards that had pictures on them—some rounded to see if he could identify the figures. Again, he could not identify anything that was curved. I spoke with the special education department and met with his mother to discuss what I had observed. The young man's mother took him to an ophthalmologist, who identified the problem as a fairly rare eye disease. He was fitted with special glasses that corrected the problem. The next day, when he came to school, he read for the first time. The other students broke out in applause.

In my classrooms, I look at an array of information on each of my students to determine if they are making progress at a rate expected for their age and maturity. I look also to see if both male and female students are making progress. I look to see that no group—whether it is a minority group, an ethnic group, or an identified group, such as at-risk students—is making less progress than expected for its age and grade level. I have found that looking at progress is a far better indicator than the average or even the median score. I have been in schools that believed their test scores were good—until we broke them down into small groups and could see that some groups were not making progress. All too often, it was either a minority group or the at-risk students that was not making progress.

When you set the standard for success in any classroom or school, set it at 100%. The first time I did that, some administrators from neighboring districts said that I was setting myself up for failure. But if you set a lower standard—let's say 80%—you have to ask, "Who are the students in the 20% group?" As a friend of mine says, "Are these 20% kids your kid or mine? Casualties are light, unless you are one of them." By the way, in the school where we set the mastery level at 100%, we reached 100% mastery in reading, 100% mastery in writing, and 99% mastery in mathematics within three years—and it was a school in which 50% of the students qualified for free or reduced lunch.

How Do We Know That Students Know?

I have often given an assessment test on a chapter or unit of study only to find that, while my students may do well on the test, they really do not know or understand the information a week later. What can we do to ensure that our students are not merely memorizing the information for the test and promptly forgetting it later? Students who do well on the test and then forget the information probably never knew it to begin with. They may have held the information in working memory long enough to write the answers on the test paper, but, because they did not process it, their brains promptly discarded the information.

Jensen (1997) uses the example of a person going to the telephone book to look up a number. He holds the information in working memory by saying it over and over while he dials the number. If a colleague walks by and asks a question while he is punching in the numbers, the chances are that he will forget the number and need to look it up again. A similar scenario happens far too often in classrooms. How can we be sure that our students really understand the information so that they can use it in the real world? Wiggins and McTighe (1998) offer six measures that we can use to determine whether our students truly know, understand, and can use the learning. Let's look at these "six facets of understanding" in light of how they can help us to build better methods of assessment.

Explain

A student who understands can explain. Being able to explain means that students can repeat what they know in their own words and can argue the critical points. It means students can add insight and reasons into the explanation based on proof; can give in-depth explanations, not simple or superficial information; will be able to explain without making common mistakes associated with the information; and will know how to make predictions based on fact rather than just opinion. Students who can explain go beyond the surface knowledge to be able to identify *why* and *how*: the student not only knows the facts of World War II, but knows why it happened. Wiggins and McTighe (1998) provide this example, "A student who can explain why steam, water, ice, though superficially different, are the same chemical substance has a better understanding of H_2O than someone who cannot."

Teaching strategies that help develop the ability to explain include:

Figure 2.1   The Prediction Tree

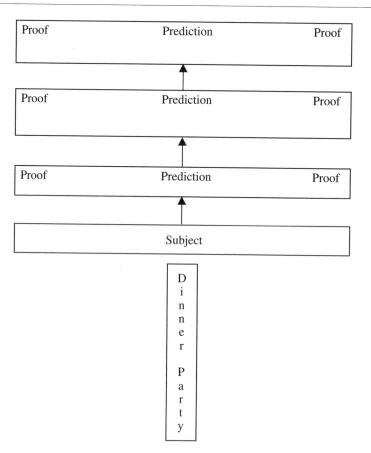

- Providing opportunities to put the learning into the words of the student. Directly teach students how to paraphrase, use bullets, and use common vocabulary.
- Asking students to summarize what they have learned that day or within the unit, then asking them to tell you how they learned the information.
- Using exercises that require students to learn to make predictions and to prove their predictions based on the preponderance of evidence, rather than on "I think" and "I feel." I use a tool called The Prediction Tree to teach my students this skill. Figure 2.1 shows an

example of how this tool could be used at the secondary level with the wonderful short story "The Dinner Party," by Mona Gardner. The same technique would also work well for elementary books.

How can we use assessment questions to help us know our students can explain? Some ideas include the following:

- Ask students to write or demonstrate with comments how they would teach a new student to solve a problem, complete an experiment, and discuss a book or reading in a step-by-step format so that the new student would fully understand.
- Follow up on initial questions, such as "How do you . . . ?" by adding a second part that asks probing questions, such as "Why?" or "How do you know?"
- Ask a question in such a way that students must prove to you that the information is correct.

Wiggins and McTighe (1998) suggest that the kinds of assessment questions that show students can explain use the following verbs: *explain, justify, generalize, predict, support, verify, prove,* and *substantiate.*

Interpret

Students who can interpret can read between the lines to give additional and plausible information. According to Wiggins and McTighe (1998), the student who can interpret "has the ability, for example, to provide historical and biographical background, thereby helping to make ideas more accessible and relevant."

Teaching strategies that help to develop interpretation include:

- Using learning logs, in which students answer given questions about the learning.

Figure 2.2   Interactive Log

Shapes with 4 sides are called? Draw three examples.	Quadrilaterals
Is this shape a trapezoid? How do you know?	Yes, it has one set of parallel sides
A rectangle can also be classified as	A quadrilateral and a parallelogram
This is an example of	A parallelogram and a quadrilateral

- Using interactive logs, which are learning logs that interact with the information by giving the students' opinions, are also a great tool for developing this technique. For example, Figure 2.2 shows an interactive log from a lesson on polynomials with the appropriate questions for students to answer in regard to the information. This tool can be used for any subject and at any grade level.
- Providing opportunities for students to contextualize the learning by putting experiences into story format or some other context familiar to the students. "To educate students for autonomous intellectual performance as adults, we must teach them to build stories and interpretations, not just passively takes in officialness. They need to see how knowledge is built from the inside" (Wiggins & McTighe, 1998).
- Providing opportunities at the end of lessons or units for students to tell not only what they have learned but what difference the learning makes.

How can we test for the ability to interpret? We can use the same tools for assessment that we use for teaching this technique. In addition, we can:

- Provide opportunities for students to write or give oral interpretations of the learning in story form.
- Provide assessments that cause students to explain how the learning relates to them personally.
- Ask "What does it mean?" or "Why does it matter?"

Apply

Students who can apply have the ability to transfer information from one format or situation to another. They can even "extend or apply what [they] know in a novel and effective way—that is, invent in the sense of innovate, as Piaget . . . discusses in *To Understand Is to Invent*" (Wiggins & McTighe, 1998). As a matter of fact, Piaget (1973) believed that understanding through application involves creative application of the knowledge. He said, "True understanding manifests itself by new spontaneous applications."

Teaching strategies that help to develop the ability to apply include:

- Modeling application by providing a real-world context for the learning and by guiding students to see how the information is used in real situations. Those students who come to class and ask "When are we ever going to use this information?" have a point: They need to know why they are learning the information.
- Using performance-based learning, which means providing opportunities for students to use the information meaningfully.
- Writing procedural objectives that require students to apply their learning in new situations, not just those provided by you. For example, after studying angles in math, talk about how angles are used in the community. Students might, for an independent project, measure the angles for angled parking in a given area (in collaboration with the Department of Public Safety, of course).

How can we test for the ability to apply knowledge? We can:

- Provide opportunities for students to create independent projects that examine the real world.
- Ask students how they will use the information.
- Ask students to name situations in which a given process or skill is used in the real world or to project future uses of the skill.
- Provide assessment opportunities that require hands-on activity.

See in Perspective

When students see in perspective, they are able to justify a position as a point of view and can place information in context. According to Wiggins and McTighe (1998), students can "Infer the assumptions upon which an idea or theory is based; know the limits as well as the power of an idea; see through an argument or language that is biased, partisan, or ideological; [and] see and explain the importance or worth of an idea."

Teaching strategies that help to develop this ability include

- Providing opportunities for students to see information in light of others' point of view. One way I teach this skill involves the Boston Tea Party. My middle school students are given invitations to a "tea party," but instead of listing their names on the invitation, I provide the name of a participant in the real event (e.g., one student might receive an invitation with the name *Quaker Francis Rotch*, another with *John Adams*, and so forth). Students get into small groups, each with all of the characters, and during the entire lesson they must take on the personality of their character (I provide information for each student on his or her character, role, attitudes, and beliefs) and explain everything in terms of their character.

- Giving students the opportunity to look at information as an outsider who is neutral to the results. For example, include a news reporter as a member of each group when you assign roles. Explain that the news reporter should be neutral, providing information on both sides of an issue, and should base the information on facts.
- Helping students to make connections between people who can interpret and the building of hypotheses. Give students the opportunity to build and prove their own hypotheses.
- Using rich media to help students understand the role of interpretation. For example, Time Life Books has a wonderful book and CD-ROM called *We Interrupt This Broadcast*, which provides images of actual moments in history as they were broadcast. Listen and watch as the newscaster interprets the event as it happens.
- Reading information from various points of view. The book *Hiroshima*, by John Hersey, was first written as a news story. Read the book to determine if he provides the information without prejudice or judgment. For elementary classrooms, the book *The True Story of the Three Pigs as Told by A. Wolfe* is a great tool to use to talk about perspectives. I use this book with secondary and college students as well, because it sounds like something right out of the morning papers: "It was all a misunderstanding; I didn't mean to do it."

How can we test for the ability to provide perspective? We can do the following:

- Ask questions that require students to look at data or information from various points of view. Does pollution look different to a factory worker than it does to an environmental organization? How? Why? What difference does it make?
- Ask students about the plausibility of an idea.

- Ask students if an action is justified or warranted.
- Ask students to rewrite a given piece from a different point of view.

Demonstrate Empathy

Students with the ability to empathize can project themselves into like situations and can see others' points of view. Even when students do not agree with the beliefs or ideas of others, they have the ability to see others' reasons for what they say or do. As Steven Covey says, these students have the ability to "seek first to understand and then to be understood."

Teaching strategies that help to develop this ability include:

- Providing opportunities for your students to put themselves in others' shoes. In science, provide background information about Einstein and the times in which he lived. Discuss what it would be like to have brilliant ideas and yet have those ideas rejected—not because of facts, but because of the time in which you live.

- Using books such as *If You Had Lived on the Mayflower* to help build empathy characteristics in elementary students.

- Involving students from an early age in the opera, the ballet, and the symphony. Listen to pieces and interpret what is happening, then take them on a field trip to the real thing.

- Discussing how early amusement rides were dangerous and how people were often injured from them. Have students design and build (through computer technology) a safe amusement ride that demonstrates what is happening to the body at various intervals.

How can we test for the ability to empathize? We can:

- Ask students what the artist was feeling or seeing while he or she was writing, painting, or playing music.

- Ask students why a person reacted as he or she did.
- Ask students how another's opinion is different from theirs, and then ask the students to explain the problem from the other person's point of view.
- Ask students to provide more than one point of view on an issue.

Reveal Self-Knowledge

A student with self-knowledge knows him- or herself. These students know their own ideas, prejudices, feelings, strengths, and weaknesses. They can identify these attributes honestly and can take criticism or feedback without feeling defensive. Such students are good at metacognition and use this process for improvement.

Teaching strategies that help to develop this ability include:

- Directly teaching students about self-knowledge, especially in light of emotional intelligence and why it is important.
- Using learning logs or other types of media to allow students to write or verbalize their thoughts and ideas.
- Using teaching techniques that lend themselves to student ideas, such as Socratic questioning or Quaker dialogues (discussed in *What Every Teacher Should Know About Effective Teaching Strategies* [Tileston, 2004a]).
- Giving students opportunities to react to the learning. Angled thinking is a tool that I like to use to introduce this concept. Figure 2.3 is an example of angled thinking on describing quadrilaterals. Students are given facts and then asked to provide their own thoughts on the same information.

How can we test for student's self-knowledge? We can do the following:

Figure 2.3   Angled Thinking

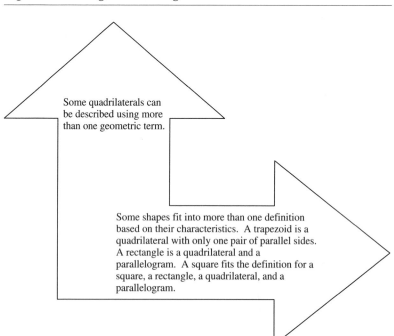

Some quadrilaterals can be described using more than one geometric term.

Some shapes fit into more than one definition based on their characteristics. A trapezoid is a quadrilateral with only one pair of parallel sides. A rectangle is a quadrilateral and a parallelogram. A square fits the definition for a square, a rectangle, a quadrilateral, and a parallelogram.

- Ask students how their background and experiences affect their beliefs about a given issue.
- Ask students to identify strengths and weaknesses within themselves.
- Use compare-and-contrast activities to help students compare themselves to others in terms of ideas, beliefs, prejudices, and so forth.
- Provide opportunities for students to self-assess their work.

USING BRAIN RESEARCH TO ENHANCE RETRIEVAL

Society tends to define smart people as those who can take in information quickly and retrieve it quickly and efficiently. With that in mind, we can increase the "smartness" of our students by enhancing their ability to take in information more efficiently and by their ability to recall the information when needed. The key to doing this lies with the memory systems of the brain.

Semantic Memory

The semantic memory is the memory system most used in classrooms, and it is the least efficient of the three activation systems in the brain—which is one of the reasons students often forget information they are taught. The semantic memory system stores and retrieves factual information, vocabulary, formulas, people, and curriculum material that deal primarily in words. Sometimes called *declarative* or *linguistic memory*, this system is activated by associations, similarities, and differences.

To learn information that is semantic, students need high intrinsic motivation and must find an association to the new information. They also need to rehearse the information to give it meaning. By rehearsal, I do not mean just rote memory techniques, but rather the use of the information in some way.

Teachers can also help students to remember information by providing a hook for the brain. For example, to help students learn the names of the Great Lakes, teachers often use the mnemonic device HOMES for the five names: Huron, Ontario, Michigan, Erie, and Superior. If you teach a subject in which students must learn a great deal of factual information, you can use some of the following teaching techniques to help your students recall information.

Mind maps. Since most students in any given classroom are visual learners, it makes sense to use visual (i.e., nonlinguistic) organizers to help them learn and remember. When being assessed by traditional test methods, students may find drawing a mind map of the information helps them to answer the test questions correctly. For example, in teaching about reptiles, the teacher might ask the students to mind map the attributes of reptiles. When being assessed by traditional paper-and-pencil test, being able to recreate the mind map on the back of the test may be helpful to many students as they answer a question on the attributes of reptiles. Mind maps are considered to be brain friendly, because at least 87% of the students in any given classroom tend to be visual, kinesthetic, or a combination of both, and the brain seems to seek patterns.

Verbalization. Pair students up and have them practice the learning by teaching the new information just covered to each other. We tend to remember 95% of what we teach to others, so this is a powerful method for putting information into long-term memory. If you like to teach by lecture, stop at intervals and have students repeat back (verbalize) the information to each other. Also, note that less than 20% of the students in any classroom are auditory learners; a straight lecture format, therefore, does not reach approximately 87% of the learners.

Questioning strategies. Questioning is important to help give relevance to the learning. Without relevance, the brain has difficulty remembering the learning. Questions might come from the teacher or from the students. Students become more literate when they have been taught to pause in their reading to ask questions and to talk to themselves or someone else about what they read.

Summarizing. Putting information into manageable chunks helps the learner to remember the information.

Practice tests or benchmarks. Help students to determine how much they know and understand through benchmark exercises or tests. The reuse of the information in another format helps the learner to remember.

Using other memory systems. Using the other two memory systems (discussed below) helps students learn and remember. For example, adding movement in the learning activates the procedural memory system, and using symbols, such as frames of reference, ties the learning to the episodic memory.

Episodic Memory

Episodic memory is location or context driven—Where were you when you learned the information? This is a powerful memory system that requires little intrinsic motivation, and when the experience is combined with emotion the learning will last indefinitely. People who were alive when President John F. Kennedy and Dr. Martin Luther King were shot can often remember where they were, who was with them, and even what they were wearing when those events happened.

This system activates memories based on places and the context of the learning. If you have ever had the experience of covering up a bulletin board on test day because information for the test is on the board, did you notice that during the test students look at the covered bulletin board when trying to recall the answers? They were activating episodic memory; their brain was remembering based on where the information was learned. We tend to do better math work in the math classroom than in the English classroom. Why? Brain researchers believe that the episodic memory is trying to activate the learning based on where it first learned it.

If you have something difficult to teach your students, try putting it up visually in your room and then see if it helps your students on those days when they need to remember the learning. If you teach a subject that requires learning facts, try combining episodic memory techniques to the semantic memory to help strengthen your students' ability to recall information.

Here are a few ideas that have worked for me and for my colleagues:

- Put the information up in the classroom so that your students see it daily.
- Change the arrangement of the classroom after each unit. For many students, that will help them to sort the information. Don't believe me? Try this experiment: The next time that you are in a meeting that lasts several

hours, move to the other side of the room after break or lunch. Most people have the experience of being in a completely different place. By the way, this is a good tool to use in discipline as well. If a student is off task, try moving him or her to the other side of the room before discussing the behavior. You are thus giving the student a "fresh start."

- Use symbols. Kay Toliver, who teachers in East Harlem, is a master at this. Kay teaches math and her students are literally on the edge of their chairs eager to learn. She often wears costumes or hats to distinguish the unit they are studying. For example, when introducing fractions, she comes dressed as a pizza chef and uses cardboard pizzas to teach about fractional parts. By doing this, she activates the episodic memory to the extent that, when her students eat pizza, they will think of fractions whether they want to or not. I use "Frames of Reference," which are cardboard frames that are passed out to groups of students when I want them to look at things from a different frame of reference. For example, for a unit on pollution, one group is given a frame that says *factory owner*, another group has a frame that says *new parent*, and a third group has a frame that says *politician*. When students need to recall information, sometimes just saying, "Remember, it was on the blue frame" is all they need to activate the memory.
- Use music. When Kay Toliver used small boxes of raisins for manipulatives in one of her math lessons, she used the music from "The California Raisin Song." You can bring in music in other ways. If you are studying World War II, bring in the sounds of the times. Music has a strong emotional effect on the brain and helps to strengthen memories.
- Use field trips to give the information a context.
- Color-code the units if you teach a great deal of vocabulary. If your school cannot afford colored paper, put a

symbol at the top of each vocabulary sheet to help students keep them straight and to give them a context for remembering.

The brain loves novelty, so anything that you can do to make the unit unique will help your students to put the information into long-term memory and to be able to retrieve it when needed.

Procedural Memory

According to Sprenger (2002), there are two ways to help students access their procedural memory. The first way is to have students practice their learning often enough that it becomes a procedure. The other is to set up procedures that create strong memories.

Anytime teachers have students do something with the learning, they are activating procedural memory. Hands-on techniques, such as lab work, manipulatives, role playing, and simulations, strengthen the learning by using procedural memory.

When teachers use performance tasks for teaching and for assessment, they are using this memory system, which is the strongest of the three systems.

TEST ANXIETY AND THE BRAIN

An important factor in assessment is the emotional response students have toward tests. If students believe that they cannot be successful, the truth is that they probably won't be successful. Students who have failed a subject or struggled through it will approach that subject with fear and dread, and being assessed in the subject will add to that anxiety. But testing is a part of the real world, whether we like it or not, so let's look at some things that the classroom teacher can do to help relieve negative emotion.

How Can We Break the Anxiety Cycle?

Let students know up-front what they have to do to be successful. I do not give any assignment to my students without first giving them a rubric or matrix that shows them exactly what they must do to be successful. This takes the personality out of grading: If a student does the work according to the rubric, the student gets the grade. It does not matter if I get along with the student; it does not matter what the student did in my classroom last year.

Rather than create a rubric for everything you do, get together with your colleagues and come up with common rubrics. Most second-grade teachers within a building are looking for the same things in assessing their students. The same is true at the secondary level with subject-area teachers. Math teachers have common attributes for which they are looking in math homework, so why not have a common rubric for math homework papers, for persuasive writing, for science experiments, etc.? When you begin to do this, you will find that the quality of the work will increase. I believe students will do quality work if someone will show them and tell them what that is.

Get away from the "gotchas." Never test students on information they have not studied or studied only in a very minor way. Remember that what is assessed should be what is taught, and what is taught should be what the written curriculum requires.

Make your classroom a place where it is okay not to know the answer. Give students many opportunities to practice the learning and to ask questions prior to being assessed. Build into your class-room benchmarks—places in the teaching learning process where you stop to see that everyone understands. Sometimes, it is asking students for a simple thumbs-up they understand. Other times, you might use a "ticket" out the door exercise, in which students must write down one thing they learned and one thing they still do not understand, which they turn in as they leave the classroom.

Observe the behavior of your students as they work on assignments to see that they do truly understand. Students learn at different paces and in different ways, so it is important to know that students have had adequate time to learn the material before assessment takes place. We are all under strict timelines to get in the material, but do not be pulled into the belief that it is more important to cover all the material than that the students understand. Don't move forward to the next unit if your students do not understand the one you have completed.

Try giving your students a subject survey at the beginning of the school year to determine their bias toward the subject matter. Eric Jensen (1997) uses the following basic questions to determine student emotions about a subject. His questionnaire uses a scale of 0 to 10, with 0 being the least and 10 being the greatest.

- When you first thought of taking this subject, your first feelings about it were (tell in your own words) . . . ?
- What are the chances you'd pick up a book or watch a movie on this topic?
- What is the likelihood that you would take up this subject/topic as a profession?
- Overall, on a scale of 0 to 10, where would you rate your interest in this subject?

Of course, this questionnaire only works if students feel they can truthfully answer without repercussions.

Move to authentic assessments. Use assessment methods that provide students with the opportunity to demonstrate their thinking and learning rather than relying solely on paper and pencil tests that rely heavily on declarative knowledge.

3

Formats for Teacher-Made Tests

Teacher-made tests and other assessments should have as their primary goal the improvement of learning. Good assessments show teachers whether students truly understand the learning and provide insight into the student's ability to use levels of thinking. Assessment should be ongoing, not something tacked on at the end of a unit of study. Assessment should be frequent enough to let the teacher and students know if they are making good progress, and they should be consistent in content application and grading. Teachers make assessments daily through informal observations, the gathering of data, and the more formal classroom test.

There are seven basic types of assessment questions or formats for teacher-made tests. Some authors divide the formats differently, but all authors use the same basic formats. In the following section, I'll provide a short definition of each type and indicate the strengths and weaknesses of each.

FORCED-CHOICE QUESTIONS

Rick Stiggins (1994) defines forced-choice assessment as

> the classic objectively scored paper-and-pencil test. The respondent is asked a series of questions, each of which is accompanied by a range of alternative responses. The respondent's task is to select either the correct or the best answer from among the options. The index of achievement is the number or proportion of questions answered correctly.

Examples of the forced choice are conventional multiple-choice, matching, alternate-choice, true/false, multiple-response, and fill-in-the-blank questions. Forced-choice questions were found to be effective to a low degree when assessing for processes, communication skills, and on nonachievement factors (such as the ability to get along with others). They had only a moderate impact on assessing declarative knowledge and thinking and reasoning skills.

Forced choice is the most commonly used format for standardized tests and is one of the poorest ways to determine whether students can use the information learned. This group of tests is called "forced" because there is generally only one right answer, so respondents are constrained by the choices offered (Stiggens, 1994). These assessments should be given when teachers want to test declarative knowledge, such as facts, dates, formulas, and general information on a topic. The next sections look at six of the most common forms of questions for forced-choice assessments.

Conventional Multiple Choice

The conventional multiple-choice format contains a *stem*, a number of *distractors*, and one correct choice. For example,

The best definition for evaluation is . . . [*stem*]

A. The collection of student data. [*distractor*]

B. The process of making a judgment. [*correct choice*]

C. The process of monitoring. [*distractor*]

According to Marzano (2000),

As tools for classroom assessment, multiple-choice items are fairly difficult and time-consuming to write. Probably the most difficult aspect of writing multiple-choice items is designing viable distracters. They must be inaccurate enough to be considered wrong by students who understand the content, but plausible enough to be selected by students who are making an educated guess.

Matching

In tests using matching questions, students are instructed to match a given item with the option that best fits. For example,

For each item below, select the option that accurately completes the statement.

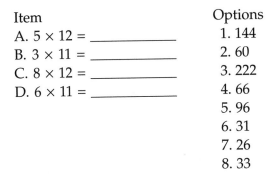

Item	Options
A. 5 × 12 = _____	1. 144
B. 3 × 11 = _____	2. 60
C. 8 × 12 = _____	3. 222
D. 6 × 11 = _____	4. 66
	5. 96
	6. 31
	7. 26
	8. 33

The main advantage to this type of format for teachers is that it takes time to create, since the correct choice for one item is a distracter for the other items. Moreover, because there are more choices than answers, students cannot use the process of elimination to find the correct answer.

Alternate Choice

Alternate-choice test questions are like multiple-choice questions, except there are only two answer options. For example,

____ 1. An (a. *assessment*, b. *evaluation*) is a process for making a judgment.

____ 2. (a. *Formative assessment*, b. *Summative assessment*) occurs before and during instruction.

This format works when the teacher wants to test for knowledge of terms and phrases. One of the biggest disadvantages is that students have a 50% chance of guessing the correct answer.

True/False

In the true/false format, students must identify a statement as accurate (*true*) or inaccurate (*false*). For example,

____ 1. Franklin D. Roosevelt was a war hero.

____ 2. Winston Churchill was a war correspondent.

____ 3. Franklin D. Roosevelt coined the phrase "V for victory."

Although this type of test gives the appearance of being easy to write, good true/false questions are actually difficult to construct. Writing false statements is much like composing distractors in multiple-choice items: They must be plausible enough to attract those students who do not really know the answer. And, like the alternate-choice questions, students have a 50% chance of guessing the correct answer.

As a word of caution to the new teacher, let me note that students may make their T's and F's look alike so that no matter what the answer choice, they can say that they wrote the correct answer. You can prevent this by having students write out the words *true* or *false*, or by having them use O's for true and X's for false.

Multiple Response

Multiple-response questions allows for more than one correct answer. For example,

Meg Byers is a first year teacher at South Middle School, where she teaches reading. She has noticed that although her students can read the vocabulary in print, they often read without understanding. Which of the following teaching tools will be helpful to her as she works with her students to improve comprehension?

1. Help students connect the reading to something they already know.

2. Have students read the information in small chunks followed by questions about what they read.

3. Keep them after school if they do not understand their work.

4. Demonstrate to students how to use self-talk as they read.
   A. 1, 2, 3, and 4
   B. 1, 2, and 4 only
   C. 1, 3, and 4 only
   D. 2 and 3 only

A variation of the multiple-response question might be,

Which of the following types of test questions has a stronger impact on assessing procedural knowledge? Place a *Y* in front of the answer(s) if they have a high effect and an *N* in front of the answer(s) that do not have a high effect on procedural knowledge.

___ Forced answer

___ Essay

___ Self-assessment

___ Performance task

___ Short written response

___ Oral reports

The advantage of this type of test is that it allows the teacher to test more than one feature of the student's knowledge. For example, in the example above, students must know the impact on assessment of all of the examples given.

Fill in the Blank

In fill-in-the-blank items, students must supply the missing word or words that make sense within a sentence. For example,

The most important function of testing is _____.

This is the easiest type of test to create, because the stem is a sentence or phrase that must be completed.

ESSAYS

Essay questions are believed to be one of the oldest forms of questions used on teacher-made tests. The Website of the National Center for Research on Evaluation, Standards, and Student Testing (CRESST, www.cresst.org) provides the following example for a written essay:

Since the start of the year, your class has been studying the principles and procedures used in chemical analysis. One of your friends has missed several weeks of class because of illness and is worried about a major exam in chemistry that will be given in two weeks. This friend asks you to explain everything that she will need to know for the exam.

Write an essay in which you explain the most important ideas and principles that your friend should understand. In your essay, you should include general concepts and specific facts you know about chemistry, and especially what you know about chemical analysis or identifying unknown substances. You should also explain how the teacher's demonstration illustrates important principles of chemistry. Be sure to show the relationships among the ideas, facts, and procedures you know.

The strength of essay-type assessments is in the stem for the essay itself. What do you want to know? Do you want to know if students understand the facts or do you want to know if they can use reasoning, problem-solving techniques, or decision making? The stem should clearly indicate what it is that you want to assess. A rubric should be provided for essay questions so that the students are clear about what it is they are being tested over.

Short Written Responses

Short written responses are really mini-essays in which students give a short answer to a given question. These types of questions are used when the teacher wants to know if the students understand the information. Some use of higher-level thinking skills may also be seen in this type of question, although it is limited somewhat by the length of the answer.

Skillfully written questions can probe beyond basic knowledge and comprehension. For example, in the short story "After Twenty Years," by O'Henry, two friends make a pact to meet 20 years after graduation to see what has happened in their lives. Jimmy stays in the area and becomes a police officer while his best friend takes off to other parts of the country and gets in trouble with the law. On the fateful night in which they are to meet, Jimmy starts down the street only to see his friend under a lamppost and recognizes him from a wanted poster. Jimmy must decide if he will arrest his friend or not. A possible short written response that would require students to think at a high level might be, "Did Jimmy use good judgment in his decisions about his friend? Why or why not? Defend your answer."

Short-Answer Questions

Short-answer questions are also mini-essays. The basic difference between a short answer question and a short response is length: A short response might be a few words or even one word to complete a prompt, whereas a short-answer question is written in whole sentence form and tends to be longer in length than short response. An example of a short-answer question at the elementary level might be, "In *The Math Curse*, by Sczescka, what are some ways the young girl was cursed by math?" At the secondary level, an example would be, "What was the major impact of the Boston Tea Party?"

These questions are best used when a teacher wants to know if students understand declarative knowledge or informational topics. These test questions are limited by the shortness of the response. Short-answer questions have a low impact on assessing processes, communication skills, and nonachievement factors. They have a moderate impact on assessing thinking and reasoning skills, and a high impact on assessing informational topics (declarative knowledge).

ORAL REPORTS

Oral reports are essays that are presented out loud. They have some of the same strengths (and weaknesses) as essays, plus they assess students' speaking ability. They are highly effective at assessing informational topics and thinking, reasoning, and communication skills. Oral reports have a moderate impact on testing process topics and a low impact on assessing nonachievement factors.

PERFORMANCE TASKS

Performance tasks require students to show what they can do with the information learned. *Performance task* is sometimes used synonymously with *authentic task*, but assessment purists will argue that performance tasks are contrived to determine whether students can use the information learned, whereas authentic tasks mirror the real world. For our purposes, the term *performance task* includes both ideas. Even a contrived task to determine if students can use information can be discussed in terms of how it might be done in the real world.

Performance tasks are ranked high in assessing accurately four of the five categories: assessing informational topics, process topics, thinking and reasoning skills, and communication skills. Performance tasks can be used to assess nonachievement factors but have a moderate impact.

TEACHER OBSERVATION

Teacher observation is an informal type of assessment used to examine a type of behavior, such as the ability to work with others. It can also be used to observe process skills, such as a student's ability to use a graph. Teacher interviews of students also come under this classification.

Teacher observation has high impact on the assessment of process topics and nonachievement factors, a moderate impact on testing informational topics, and a low impact in assessing thinking and reasoning as well as communication skills.

STUDENT SELF-ASSESSMENT

Student self-assessment is the most underused form of class-room assessment. Students assess their own thinking, work, processes, and learning in this format. Student self-assessment has a high reliability in all five of the assessment categories: informational topics, process topics, thinking and reasoning skills, communication skills, and nonachievement.

Testing for Intelligence

What is intelligence? Defining intelligence is an endeavor that has long consumed the human mind. In ancient Greece, Plato believed that humans were largely ignorant and that the knowledge they acquired was only an insignificant abstraction of a much larger and perfect truth. Plato claimed he could only be considered smart because he was aware of his own ignorance.

—Silver, Strong, and Perini
So Each May Learn

We have long held that an intelligence quotient (IQ) is a number derived by dividing a child's "mental age" (derived from his or her score on an intelligence test) by the child's actual age. IQ is based on the principle that children who score well on intelligence tests have mental ability comparable to older children who are only average. A child who performs as expected for his or her age has an IQ of 100; a child with mental ability considerably higher than his or her age might have an IQ of 130. The term *IQ* is no longer used as frequently as it once was, but intelligence tests continue to be scored using the familiar scale.

What, then, is intelligence? Does the definition change depending on the culture? Can it be calculated using a single measure, as with the intelligence tests so often administered in schools? These and similar questions have been explored over the years, and they have led to Howard Gardner's conclusion that intelligence is not a single measure but rather a measure of many phenomena. As Gardner (1983) explains,

> I performed a "thought" experiment in which I imagined going into many different cultures and trying to identify, in each, its developed roles or "end states"—abilities highly prized in that culture, and really important for its survival. As part of the experiment, I thought about religious leaders, shamans, seers, mothers, fathers, dancers, surgeons, sculptors, hunters, businessmen, and so forth. I put myself to the challenge of coming up with a notion of cognition that could give a better account of how the human organism can become highly competent in these very diverse kinds of capacities.

The 20th century was a time of great changes in the way that we look at intelligence and learning. Even as our understanding of human cognition becomes more scientific and precise, our initial question remains: What is human intelligence?

Gardner (1983) defines intelligence as:

- The ability to solve problems that one encounters in real life.
- The ability to generate new problems to solve.
- The ability to make something or offer a service that is valued within one's culture.

In his groundbreaking book *Frames of Mind* (1983), Gardner changed the way that we look at intelligence. Silver, Strong, and Perini (2000) assert that the new view of intelligence that emerged from Gardner's recognizes that:

- Intelligence can be developed; it is not fixed at birth.
- Intelligence is not measured by a single number as in a traditional IQ test but is measured best during a performance or problem-solving process. This means that we do not measure intelligence based on declarative or factual information but on procedural information (i.e., what can the student do with the knowledge?).
- Intelligence can be measured in more than one way.
- Intelligence is measured in real-world context rather than the isolated context of standard IQ tests.
- Intelligence is meant to measure the varied ways that a student is intelligent rather than a single measure that says the student will be successful or not.

While Gardner began with the identification of seven types of intelligence—and then added an eighth—the belief is that there are more intelligences yet to be discovered (e.g., is there a sixth sense and how might it be measured?). Let's look at Gardner's eight intelligences and examine how the classroom teacher can identify and increase students' intelligence level in each.

TYPES OF INTELLIGENCE

Verbal-Linguistic Intelligence

As the name implies, people with strong verbal-linguistic intelligence are adept at using words, whether in written or spoken language. They tend to learn best when there are auditory teaching activities. This does not mean that they learn best by lecture, because these students also like to talk to one another to discuss the information in order to make it personal. According to Silver et al. (2000), verbal-linguistic learners "learn best when they can speak, listen, read or write."

At a young age, students who are word smart like to tell jokes, stories, and tall tales. They usually have a good memory for words and like to play word games. Their vocabulary may be advanced for their age, and they are usually good communicators. These students like to read and write.

At an advanced stage, these students are able to express themselves in various creative writing forms and can create original stories. They are usually good public speakers and can use various figures of speech, such as metaphor, simile, and hyperbole.

In the classroom, verbal-linguistic students love anything that has to do with speaking, writing, or reading. The classroom teacher can enhance this intelligence by adding discussions in whole groups, small groups, or pairs. Teachers can also use journal writing or learning logs. Learning logs can be used at the beginning of a lesson to provide opportunities for students to identify what they already know about a topic, or they may be used throughout the lesson to identify learning. Finally, teachers can promote verbal-linguistic intelligence by using writing throughout the curriculum. Writing is not just for the English language arts classroom but should be a part of every classroom. We know that when students truly understand the learning, they can explain it to someone else. As a departure from the traditional methods of assessment, ask students to explain a problem, formula, scientific test, or activity that they have studied as if they were teaching it to someone else.

Logical-Mathematical Intelligence

Logical-mathematical intelligence is the basis of the hard sciences and all types of mathematics. People who use logical-mathematical intelligence emphasize the rational: They are usually good at finding patterns, establishing cause-and-effect relationships, conducting controlled experiments, and sequencing. Generally, they think in terms of concepts and questions, and they love to put ideas to the test.

At a young age, logical-mathematical students like strategy games, math activities, and logic puzzles. They ask questions about how things work. These students may exhibit the ability to use higher-level thinking skills at an early age.

At an advanced stage, these students can link various mathematical operations for complex problem solving. They know how to find unknown quantities in problem solving. They are good at using both inductive and deductive reasoning processes, can perform logical thinking, and can use standard math proofs.

In the classroom, these students will enjoy activities that require finding patterns, making calculations, forming and testing hypotheses, and, using the scientific method, deduction, and induction. Teachers can add to the development of this intelligence by using deductive and inductive reasoning and by teaching students to make comparisons to formulate a hypothesis or to look for trends. Math puzzles are also a great way to enhance logical-mathematical intelligence.

Spatial Intelligence

Spatial intelligence involves a high capacity for perceiving, creating, and re-creating pictures and images. Photographers, artists, engineers, architects, and sculptors all use spatial intelligence. People who are spatially intelligent are keenly perceptive of even slight visual details; can usually sketch ideas out with graphs, tables, or images; and are often able to convert words or impressions into mental images. Spatially intelligent people also think in images and have a keen sense of location and direction.

At a young age, students with this intelligence can see clear mental pictures of the learning and may daydream in the classroom. They like puzzles and mazes, and they understand more from pictures than from words while reading. These students may doodle on their papers or anything else that is handy and usually like art activities.

At an advanced stage, these students may understand how to make something from a blueprint, pattern, or diagram. They can read and create maps, and seem to have a good understanding of abstract spatial images, such as geometry. They may use various art forms and understand spatial relationships of patterns.

In the classroom, spatially intelligent students like projects that give them an opportunity to represent ideas visually, to create mental images, and to use musical intelligence. Teachers can enhance this intelligence by adding visuals to the learning. An important way to do this is to add concept maps such as the mind map or the attribute wheel.

Bodily-Kinesthetic Intelligence

Bodily-kinesthetic intelligence is related to the physical self and the manipulation of one's own body. Those who are kinesthetically intelligent can generally handle objects or make precise bodily movements with relative ease. Their tactile sense is usually well developed, and they enjoy physical challenges and pursuits. These learners learn best by doing, moving, and acting things out.

At a young age, students with this intelligence show an early aptitude for running, jumping, and sports activities. They may have difficulty sitting still in class and may tap their pencil, fidget, or move around in their seats. These students like to take things apart and put them back together, and they are often the student who wants to build a model for a project.

At an advanced stage, students with aptitude in this intelligence exhibit an ability to perform in a variety of invention activities or to make something new. They have creative and expressive body movements and may be athletic in sports, gymnastics, or dance. These students may also be very good at role playing or mime.

In the classroom, these learners like projects that involve strength, speed, flexibility, hand-eye coordination, and balance. Teachers who add movement to the learning are not only helping to develop this intelligence but are helping the brain to store the information in a more user-friendly format than the semantic memory pathway. Manipulatives, building and using models, and hands-on activities are just some of the ways that we can use this intelligence in the classroom.

Musical Intelligence

Musical intelligence is the ability to produce melody and rhythm, as well as to understand, appreciate, and form opinions about music. People able to sing in key, keep tempo, analyze musical forms, or create musical expression exhibit musical intelligence. Musically intelligent people are sensitive to all types of nonverbal sound and the rhythms of everyday noise.

At a young age, these students may exhibit an ability to know when music is off-key, and they can remember melodies. These students usually like to play a musical instrument or sing. These students can also sing songs they have learned outside the classroom and may tap their pencil or move their foot to a melody in their minds.

At an advanced level, students who have musical intelligence will have an understanding of and appreciation for different kinds of music. They can use music to express ideas, thoughts, and feelings. They will also usually understand the language of music, such as musical symbols and terms.

In the classroom, these students love listening to music, singing, and playing an instrument. They can come up with jingles, raps, and songs to add to the learning. Music has a dramatic emotional impact on the brain and can enhance learning by adding emotion. When studying a period in history, add the sounds of the times through music to the learning.

Interpersonal Intelligence

Interpersonal intelligence is at work in people who are naturally social. Interpersonally intelligent people work well with others and are quite sensitive to slight variations in people's moods, attitudes, and desires. Often, interpersonally intelligent people are friendly and outgoing. Most people with this intelligence know how to gauge, identify with, and read to the temperaments of others. They are generally excellent team players and managers, and they learn best when they can relate to other people.

At a young age, these students may exhibit a natural ability as a leader and will enjoy socializing with friends. They like to belong to clubs or other groups and to play group games. They usually show concern for others and may be good at giving advice to their friends.

At a more advanced stage, interpersonally intelligent students will be good at conflict management and will understand the various group dynamics taking place. They are sensitive to others, and they want fairness in respect to others' beliefs, motivations, cultural values, and social norms. These students are usually good at cooperative and/or collaborative learning activities.

In the classroom, these students enjoy projects that include group activities, such as cooperative learning or peer tutoring. If you are teaching a lesson in which you must talk for long periods of time, you can enhance interpersonal intelligence by breaking up the lecture and using the following technique:

1. Place students in pairs and ask them to decide who is partner A and who is partner B.

2. After you have provided a chunk of information, ask partner A to tell partner B everything that you have said in the last few minutes.

3. Next, ask partner B to tell partner A everything that they remember that partner A left out.

A variation of this strategy, which I use for secondary students, is to place students into small groups of 3 or 4 and assign each group a different responsibility (e.g., one group can be responsible for summarizing the information you present, another group for asking questions, and a third for bulleting important points). If the information to be presented is complex, you might divide up the topics by groups, so that one group is responsible for summarizing topic A, one group for summarizing topic B, and so forth.

Intrapersonal Intelligence

Intrapersonal intelligence is the ability to gain access to one's own feelings and emotional states. Intrapersonally intelligent people usually choose to work on their own, as they use and trust their self-understanding to guide them. They are in touch with their inner feelings and are able to form realistic goals and conceptions of themselves.

At an early age, these students usually prefer working alone and have high self-esteem. They display a sense of independence and have a realistic sense of their own strengths.

At an advanced stage, intrapersonally intelligent students have high emotional intelligence and are good at using higher-order thinking to work through problems. They are actively exploring and forming personal beliefs, values, goals, and philosophies and are usually interested in self-improvement.

In the classroom, these students like goal setting, monitoring their own work, and engaging in reflection activities. Reflection activities are an important part of any lesson. Teachers can help students develop good reflection tools by providing the general ideas for them. For example, a PMI (Positive–Minus–Interesting) tool may be used after a lesson to help students see and understand what they have learned. Under the P heading, students write the major points of what they have learned today; under the M, they write questions about or problems with the learning; and under the I, they write their thoughts and ideas about the learning. Another tool, called *angled thinking*, is a great way for students to analyze their own thoughts about the learning. In this activity, students transfer information being studied to their own lives (an example of angled thinking was provided in Chapter 2).

Naturalistic Intelligence

Naturalistic intelligence is found in those who are highly attuned to the world of plants and animals, as well as to geography and natural objects like rocks, clouds, and stars. People who have a high naturalist intelligence love to be outdoors and tend to notice patterns, features, and anomalies in the ecological settings they encounter. They are adept at using these patterns and features to classify and categorize natural objects and living things. Those with the naturalist intelligence show an appreciation for, and a deep understanding of, the environment.

At a young age, these students are happiest when outdoors and show a high interest in nature. They like and appreciate animals and are interested in conservation. They seem to understand patterns of nature, such as weather, and may have a sense that the weather is changing based on what they observe in nature. They usually like science experiments that are related to nature.

At an advanced stage, naturalist students will know the names of plants, animals, and their habitats. They will be keenly aware of natural patterns and will use that information to make observations about changes in the earth, weather, and so forth. Older students have the ability to make distinctions and form classes among plants, animals, and other parts of the natural environment and man-made objects.

In the classroom, these students like to identify and classify living things and natural objects. The attribute wheel used in spatial relationships is a great way to identify attributes in order to better classify them. While this information is important to know in terms of strengths and weaknesses of naturalistically intelligent students, it is also vital in helping students to choose projects and products that are meaningful to them.

USING THE INTELLIGENCES TO ENHANCE CLASSROOM ACTIVITIES

Providing a variety of activities in the classroom that address various intelligences will not only help motivate students to learn but will also help develop those intelligences where there are areas of weaknesses. Following are some ideas from Silver et al. (2000).

Targeting the Development of Specific Intelligences

At the elementary level, teachers target specific intelligences through activity centers—stations set up stations throughout the classroom with learning tools relating to each intelligence. Silver et al. (2000) offer some examples:

> A verbal-linguistic center might include books and word processors, whereas a bodily-kinesthetic center would include manipulatives and hands-on items. Further, activity centers may be open-ended giving students freedom to choose their own endeavors, or they may be topic-specific by providing an activity that relates specifically to instructional objectives. For example, at the spatial center you might ask students to create a comic strip that shows how Shirley Temple Wong adjusted to life in America in the book *In the Year of the Boar and Jackie Robinson.*

Differentiating Instruction Through Multiple Intelligences

By using a variety of teaching tools a teacher is more likely to teach to students' strengths. Silver et al. (2000) use the example of a lesson on endangered species to show how multiple intelligences can be used:

- Verbal-linguistic students can be involved in class discussions and developing a newsletter on endangered species.
- Logical-mathematical students can analyze endangered species case studies, determining the causes of endangerment and comparing and contrasting two endangered species, such as the tiger and the panda.
- Spatial students can use video clips from *Saving Nature* to understand endangered animals and can sketch animals from the endangered species list.
- Bodily-kinesthetic students can engage in role-playing activities and take a field trip to a wildlife preserve.

Table 4.1   Using Multiple Intelligences for Project Ideas

Project Idea	Intelligence
Acrostic poem	Verbal-linguistic
Advice letter	Verbal-linguistic
Autobiography	Verbal-linguistic
Chart/graph	Logical-mathematical or spatial
Choral reading	Verbal-linguistic and interpersonal
Collage	Spatial
Diorama	Spatial
Eyewitness report	Verbal-linguistic and interpersonal
Journal	Intrapersonal
Map	Logical-mathematical and spatial
Model	Bodily-kinesthetic and spatial
Song, rap, or jingle	Musical
Timeline	Spatial
Demonstration	Bodily-kinesthetic
Simulation	Bodily-kinesthetic
Play	Bodily-kinesthetic and verbal-linguistic
Nature walk	Naturalistic
Classification of animals	Naturalistic

- Intrapersonal students can explore such questions as "How would it feel to be an endangered species?" and "Why is nature important to you?"
- Musical students can listen to a folk song on an endangered species.
- Interpersonal student can work in groups on the newsletter and on a group project on raising awareness.

Providing Choices Through Activities and Independent Projects

Table 4.1 shows a list of independent project ideas that appeal to the different intelligences.

Performance
Tasks

P erformance tasks require students to use the information learned to construct a response. Here are some examples of performance tasks from the National Assessment of Educational Progress:

- Students are asked to describe what occurs when a drop of water is placed on each of seven different types of building materials. Next, they are asked to predict what will happen to a drop of water as it is placed on the surface of unknown material, which is sealed in a plastic bag so that students can examine it but not test it.
- Students are given a sample of three different materials and an open box. The samples differ in size, shape, and weight. The students are asked to determine which box would weigh the least (and the most) if it were filled completely with materials A, B, or C.

While these tasks require the use of procedural knowledge (what can students do with the information), they are not real-world tasks. To move to real-world tasks, a student might be asked to do the following:

- Use information from your unit on current events to write a persuasive letter to the editor of your local newspaper citing your stand on stem cell research. (For secondary-level students.)
- Use the information from your unit on weather to write a letter to the meteorologist at the local newspaper and make predictions about the weather patterns for your town for the next three months. Ask for feedback about your predictions.

The difference between these two exercises is that, in the first set of questions, students are asked to perform tasks that will give the teacher insight into their thinking and reasoning as well as into their ability to use learned information. In the second set of exercises, the teacher gains the same information but the stakes are higher, because the students are responding to real-world people and situations. Both are powerful exercises, and the decision on which to use is a matter of personal choice for the teacher. Personally, I believe that we can use contrived exercises to teach skills and to glean information, and we can then help students to identify how those exercises might look in the real world. We can also add the element of the real-world exercise, but both kinds of exercises are valuable. The key is to ask, "Do the students understand the connection to the real world?" not "Is this real world?"

PORTFOLIOS

Portfolios have received a great deal of recognition in the last few years as the new "in" thing to do. Studies by Mid-continent Regional Education Laboratory (McREL) under the direction of Bob Marzano (1998) indicate that portfolios themselves do not have a profound effect on student progress; rather, it is the use of constructive, precise, and frequent feedback that has the strong effect on student learning. One might conclude from this information that the quality of portfolios is directly attributed to the quality of the feedback provided to students.

It should be noted here that portfolios, which contain samples of students work over time and should show growth, are a form of performance tasks. While they were originally used to show products in writing and the arts, they are also used to show progress in thinking over time. For example, Marzano (2000) describes the kinds of information that might be included in a mathematics portfolio:

- Samples of word problems used throughout a semester or year with information for the student about how he or she solved the problems.
- Samples of mathematical concepts studied with notes from the student explaining the concepts and how they are used.
- The student's self-evaluation of his or her understanding of concepts, strategies, or algorithms that have been covered in class along with examples.

TEACHER OBSERVATION

Teachers are constantly watching students work and making decisions based on those observations. Observations are used for gathering information not only about the cognitive work of students but about behavior as well. How are students doing in regard to their performance tasks? Do they show evidence of high energy throughout the project? Do they quit when they encounter a problem in the process? Do they have a plan, and are they able to monitor and adjust that plan as needed to complete the task? Teacher observation is probably one of the best ways to identify such nonachievement factors as effort, behavior, and attendance to detail.

STUDENT SELF-ASSESSMENT

Considered to be one of the strongest tools in leading students to improvement and yet one of the least-used tools, student self-assessment can be employed for a variety of purposes. Metacognition of the learning—that is, thinking about the learning that has taken place—is a strong, brain-compatible way to make the learning meaningful and reassess the learning. Students should ask thoughtful questions, such as, What did I like about this project? What went well? What were the problems encountered? What will I do differently next time? These kinds of questions lead to goal setting and to the use of higher-level thinking, such as evaluation, analysis, and synthesis.

Students should be given opportunities to monitor their own work and to evaluate their performance tasks especially in regard to following a plan, being able to make adjustments as needed throughout the project, and on the quality of their work.

INDEPENDENT OR GROUP PROJECTS

There was a time in my teaching career when I would assign independent projects to my students with the strict instructions that I wanted the products to be at a quality level. I soon learned that what I consider to be a quality product and what the students considered to be quality were not necessarily the same thing. No teacher wants to take the time involved in independent projects only to receive work that is far below the abilities of the students.

Projects are just one example of procedural knowledge, but they are an important example. Over the years, I have put together a formula for student projects. This formula can also apply to any procedural task that you assign your students. Here is a breakdown of my formula:

1. Students identify the topic of their project and provide goals and benchmarks for the project.

2. Students are given a matrix or rubric to show them exactly what they will be evaluated on and what I mean by "quality product."

3. I provide a wide variety of project ideas to my students. They may use one of the ideas that I give or they may come up with their own, but it must be of the same quality.

My project ideas are based both on where I think my students are in terms of Bloom's Taxonomy and on various media (e.g., written, oral, kinesthetic). When I look at student projects in terms of Bloom's Taxonomy, I am attempting to identify where my students are in terms of depth. On which level are my students capable of working? Some years I have students who don't even know how to research for basic information. For those students, the lower levels of Bloom's serve as a starting point. Some years I have students who are already working at the analysis or synthesis level. To ask them to perform a task at the knowledge or comprehension level would be an insult and would have the appearance of "busy work." I have devised a formula for determining the levels of learning and the procedures for independent projects using Bloom's Taxonomy as my guide.

BLOOM'S TAXONOMY

Knowledge Level

Knowledge is the lowest level of Bloom's Taxonomy. In order to produce a project at this level, a student does not have to fully understand what the project is about. For example, a timeline would be an example of a project at the knowledge level. A student could put together a timeline of the events that lead to World War II without fully understanding the significance of the events. Projects at the knowledge level might include collecting information, making observations, or recalling factual information.

Knowledge-level abilities include:

- Defining
- Listing information

- Providing facts
- Asking *what, who, when,* and *where*
- Labeling

Examples of possible knowledge-level projects include:

- Creating a collection of insects with appropriate labels.
- Providing a 25-card fact file on an assigned person, place, or thing.
- Writing a "help wanted" ad for the witch in *Piggie Pie* to help her get the ingredients for her pie.

This is a low level of understanding because it requires very few of the seven facets of understanding described in Chapter 2. Some of these assignment ideas are more difficult than others because they require time (the fact file) and creativity (the help-wanted ad), but they are not complex, and they do not require a great deal of understanding.

Comprehension Level

At the comprehension level, students take factual information and demonstrate understanding. The amount of understanding required determines the complexity of the project.

Comprehension-level skills include the ability to:

- Understand information
- Grasp meaning
- Translate knowledge into new context
- Interpret facts, compare, contrast
- Order, group, and infer causes
- Predict consequences

Activities that demonstrate comprehension-level thinking include:

- Summarizing
- Describing

- Interpreting
- Comparing and contrasting
- Predicting
- Making associations
- Distinguishing among items
- Estimating
- Differentiating

Project ideas include having students dramatize a meeting between two leaders in history that includes keys to their personalities or having students prepare a notes book for an incoming student into the class by summarizing important vocabulary or formulas.

Application Level

The application level means that the student not only knows the information, she or he understands it and can use it in a meaningful way. Again, the degree to which the student can use it uniquely determines the amount of complexity in the project. Is the student simply using the information in the same way that it was presented in the classroom, or is he or she applying it to a real-world context outside the classroom?

Application-level abilities include:

- Drawing conclusions and generalizing
- Understanding the main idea
- Comprehension
- Understanding the problem
- Converging on an answer

Questions and activities that demonstrate application-level understanding include:

- Drawing a conclusion from given information
- Asking "What are the main points?"
- Explain in their own words

- Identifying the single most important idea in a unit
- Identifying patterns
- Applying a rule

An example of a project at this level might be to identify an area of the country that is prone to tornadoes, chart the patterns that occur in the weather prior to each incident of tornado activity, and apply that information to making predictions about future weather patterns.

Analysis Level

At the analysis level, students are able to find information, understand it, use it, and can break it down into manageable parts.

Students who can analyze can:

- Classify, group, sort, and categorize
- Rank order
- Compare and contrast data
- Sequence data
- Diagram, chart, graph, and make tables
- Visualize
- Determine part-whole relationships
- Determine cause and effect
- Explain space-time relationships
- Understand function relationships
- Interpret information
- Categorize, sort, arrange, and rearrange

Questions and activities that demonstrate analysis include:

- Asking "In what order did X occur?"
- Making a chart, diagram, or graph
- Arranging from *most important* to *least important*
- Comparing and contrasting
- Asking "How are they alike and different?"

- Asking "How does A effect B?"
- Asking "How could you group/classify A?"
- Showing how the parts relate to the whole

An example of a project at this level might be to create a compare-and-contrast chart on the characteristics of presidents. Questions to consider in making such a chart might include, Why did we elect George Washington to be the first president of the United States and not one of the rabble-rousers who were pouring tea over the sides of ships? Why did we choose someone who was very structured? (Perhaps we needed structure at that time?) Students might then be asked to use the information to make predictions about a national election based on the personalities of the candidates.

Synthesis Level

At the synthesis level, students can do all of the levels below synthesis, and they can create a product that is their own, not a copy of something else.

Students who work at the synthesis level can:

- Invent, create, and synthesize
- Devise a plan
- Infer, predict, and hypothesize
- Apply and use ideas

Questions and activities that demonstrate synthesis include:

- Making a plan to do something
- Apply an idea to a new situation
- Predicting what will happen
- Hypothesizing what will happen if X occurs
- Asking "What should you do if X occurs?"
- Creating
- Inventing a way to do something

- Designing a solution to prove/show/improve something
- Identifying when, in the real world, one would use this information
- Asking "What if?"
- Identifying how many different ways one can do X

Following are some sample assignments from www.engine-uity.com:

- Invent a system for recognizing and understanding ambiguity and paradox. Teach your method to your class.
- Create a board game, which organizes information about explorers, expeditions, trade items, and national goals.

Evaluation Level

At the evaluation level, students can perform at all of the lower levels, plus they can make evaluations about the learning. Students who work at the evaluation level can:

- Value new learning
- Evaluate, judge, and look back

Questions and activities that demonstrate the ability to evaluate include:

- Identifying if the day's lesson was valuable and explaining why
- Asking "How could this have been done better?"
- Asking "Do you believe this is a good idea? Why?"
- Forming an opinion and explaining it
- Identifying the best way to do X
- Asking "Are you satisfied with this answer/solution/plan?"
- Asking "What information convinced you?"
- Asking "Why do you believe your prediction was incorrect?"
- Asking "Are you satisfied with the way you approached the problem?"

Table 5.1   Applying the Formula

	Level	*Topic*	*Product*
Knowledge	Label	Parts of a plant	Sketch
	List	Freedoms in Bill of Rights	Chart
	Identify	Food groups	Model
Comprehension	Interpret	Rate of inflation	Oral report
	Sequence	Steps from an idea to a bill	Timeline
	Collect	Examples	Role play
	Show	Principle of estimation	Mind map
Application	Demonstrate	Patterns	Tessellations
	Reorganize	A chapter from a text	Teach
	Develop	A book report	Brochure
Analysis	Break down	Component parts	Demonstrate
	Simplify	Formulas	Booklet
Synthesis	Create	A new song from an old melody	Performance
	Predict	Election results	Monograph
Evaluation	Judge	A historical decision	Letter to editor

Sample projects from www.engine-uity.com include the following:

- Insects are the most successful invertebrates, and man is the most successful vertebrate. Select which one—man or insect—is the most successful animal with regard to adapting to environmental changes. Defend your choice in a written essay.
- Assess the importance of Harrison's Chronometer in terms of navigation. Write an illustrated, persuasive article for the *Navigator Bulletin*.

APPLYING THE FORMULA

With this information on the levels of Bloom's Taxonomy, a formula can be applied to determine the level, the topic, and the product for a given project. Table 5.1 shows how to apply the formula by choosing the level of difficulty, the topic, and then the possible products.

6

Using a Matrix
or Rubric

J ensen (1997) says, "Pop quizzes should be banned. They
   create stressful, adversarial (teacher vs. student) relationships, provide little useful information, and are often used to
give students a wake-up call by showing them how little they
know."

If we are truly to move our students toward quality work
and quality assessments, we must tell them up front what we
expect and what they must do to be successful. Because over
87% of the learners are visual (Jensen, 1997), the information
on expectations should be in writing. The preferred method is
by matrix or rubric.

Using a Matrix to
Describe the Desired Results

A matrix simply lists the component parts of a product or
learning exercise on the left-hand side and the attributes that
make it quality on the right-hand side. The center may be
used for point values when there is a difference in the weight
of points for the different component parts. Table 6.1 is an

Table 6.1   Matrix for Homework

Criteria	Attributes
All problems are worked.	• Steps are followed correctly. • All work is shown. • Work is checked.
Understanding of mathematics is evident.	• Explains work thoroughly. • Is able to justify answers. • Is able to explain the process to others.
Work is turned in at a timely interval.	• Work is submitted on time. • Work is complete.
Work is legible.	• Work is neat and legible. • Work can be easily seen and understood.

example of a simple matrix for math homework. Table 6.2 is an example of a simple matrix for a timeline project.

One of the basic differences between a matrix and a rubric is that whereas a rubric lists the attributes at different levels of learning, the matrix assumes there is only one level of learning. I use a matrix when I expect only one level of learning, and that is a quality level. When teaching in a classroom of diverse learners who are working on different levels of complexity, a rubric is more appropriate.

USING AND BUILDING RUBRICS

Rubrics are a little more complicated to put together precisely because they describe different levels of learning. One of the simplest rubrics is the 4 × 4 grid in which there are four levels of learning and four criteria for grading. Table 6.3 is an example of such a 4 × 4 rubric.

Wiggins and McTighe (1998) argue that a good rubric will distinguish between shallow thinking and more complex

Table 6.2   Matrix for Timeline

TIMELINE

Parts (Essentials)	Points	Attributes
Title	☒	Appropriate
	☒	Concise
Line	☒	Ruled
	☒	Topic is represented
	☒	Easy to read
Time increments	☒	Uniformly sized
	☒	Clearly visible
	☒	At equal intervals
	☒	Subunits of time for important events
Labels	☒	Legibly printed
	☒	Uniformly sized
	☒	Key events represented
Illustrations	☒	Match the theme
	☒	Appropriate
Credits	☒	Alphabetized
	☒	Visible from the front
Overall appearance	☒	Completed neatly

Table 6.3   Rubric for Math Work in Classroom Setting

Mathematician	Emerging	Beginning	Novice
Shows a mature understanding of math facts. Is able to work all problems successfully and to show work appropriately.	Shows a growing understanding of mathematics. Is able to explain and verify work on a limited basis.	Shows some understanding of mathematics. Is able to work some problems and has a narrow understanding of how the problems were worked.	Shows a simplistic or naive understanding of mathematics. Is not able to work problems successfully.
Shows a thorough ability to interpret and analyze math problems and to provide reasons that are fully supported and verified.	Can give some reasons for his or her work. Can interpret and analyze to some degree but not always. Can explain with prompts.	Has a vague idea of how the math works and can explain on a superficial level.	Shows inability to interpret or analyze math problems. Does not understand how the math works.
Turns work in on time, sometimes ahead of time, with all work shown and in neat order. Poses appropriate and thoughtful questions about the learning. Knows limitations.	Turns work in on time, but with some mistakes and noted erasures. Does ask for help most of the time when needed.	Work is sometimes on time. No consistency in the quality of the work or in the student's understanding of his or her limitations.	Work is often late or not turned in at all. Fails to ask for help when needed or relies on other students for help.

thinking (as we examined in Chapter 2). They provide the following questions as a guide in deciding the levels of thinking in a rubric: "What is the difference between a simple and a sophisticated proof in mathematics? What is the difference between a complex and simple analysis of a literary text or historical event?"

Once the rubric—or matrix—has been developed, it should be shared with students, explained, and used consistently during grading. For example, if I create a rubric but don't follow my own criteria in grading, the rubric has no meaning, and students will not pay attention the next time I use one. Because I believe that more students would work at a quality level if they know what their teachers meant by "quality," I believe this one tool can raise the learning level of students significantly.

7

Building Aligned Assessments

I n the previous chapters, you have learned the vocabulary used with assessment, the kinds of questions used in making tests, and the importance of alignment of national, state, and local curricula with what is taught in the classroom. You are ready to put all of this information to work for you in your classroom.

In this chapter, you will choose an objective from your curriculum, tie it to your state goals, and develop a test for use in the classroom. You will also develop a matrix to assess the learning and then analyze data to make classroom decisions. There are six steps in building assessments, beginning with choosing the goals for the learning.

STEP ONE:
CHOOSING CLASSROOM GOALS

As discussed in Chapter 1, we will begin this process with the end in mind.

Choose a unit of study that you will be teaching in your classroom. For example, at the elementary level, you may be about to introduce a unit on the sounds associated with the letter D. You may have planned to use the wonderful spoof of Cinderella called *Dinorella*, by Pamela Duncan Edwards.

Once you have identified the topic, you are ready to write the objectives. For the lesson on the letter sound D, I would write the lesson and objectives like this:

Title of Lesson: The letter D

Local Objective: 1.8—Students will use letter-sound knowledge to decode written language.

State Objective: 1.7A—Name and identify each letter of the alphabet

1.7B—Understand that written words are composed of letters that represent sounds.

STEP TWO:
WRITING THE OBJECTIVES

What do you want your students to know and be able to do at the end of the unit? What students know is considered to be *declarative knowledge*, and what they can do is *procedural knowledge*. How will you know that students understand? Remember the six facets of understanding from Wiggins and McTighe (1998): When we truly understand, we do the following:

- *Explain* the information learned.
- *Interpret* the information and add personal knowledge to it.
- *Apply* the information to other contexts.
- *Have perspective* so that we not only see the big picture, but can also make critical judgments.

- *Empathize* with others and understand that other people have opinions and points of view.
- *Have self-knowledge* so that we know when we do not understand.

Write at least three declarative objectives (what students will know) and three procedural objectives (what students will be able to do) for your lesson.

STEP THREE: MONITORING STUDENT UNDERSTANDING

How will you know if students understand? For this step, you will need to list some ways that you will monitor student understanding. Some of those may be formative and take the form of observation, checklists, practices, or benchmarks. Others should also be summative and take the form of assessments.

STEP FOUR: CREATING A RUBRIC

The next step is to create a rubric. A rubric is a written guide of how you will assess student learning and understanding. It should include both declarative and procedural assessments.

On the left side of the rubric, list the criteria that you will use to evaluate student learning. In the rows, list the ways you will identify whether students meet—or exceed—the criteria given in that row. If you need help in deciding how to word this information, you can refer to the Discovery.com Website (www.school.discovery.com/schrockguide/assess.html), which includes hundreds of ideas for creating rubrics.

You may also want to go to this Website to practice making rubrics, because it provides step-by-step guidelines for making simple to complex rubrics. Start with a simple rubric that has only one criterion, then move to one with two and then three criteria.

Table 7.1   Analysis of Test Questions

Student Names	Gender (M/F)	Ethnicity	At Risk	Question 1	Question 2
Martin, A.	M	A	Yes	X	O
Marquez, M.	M	H		X	O
North, S.	F	NA		O	X
Pei, K.	F	A	Yes	X	X

Note: Ethnicity—A = Anglo; H = Hispanic; NA = Native American

Questions—X = incorrect answer; O = correct answer.

STEP FIVE:
PREPARING ASSESSMENT TOOLS

You are now ready to prepare your assessment tools. These tools might be formal, as in a written assessment instrument, or they may be informal, as in teacher observations. It is advisable that you include more than one assessment type.

STEP SIX:
ASSESSING THE ASSESSMENT

Choose an assessment tool that you have used in the past. How successful was the assessment in measuring whether you met your objectives? Using the chart provided in Table 7.1 as a guide, list the first names or initials of students in the classroom and indicate by question number which questions were missed and which were answered correctly. Examine the data in your graph for bias and to determine student understanding. Did one group test better than others? If so, why? Is there a question that most of the class missed? If so, analyze why you think that happened. Was the question clear? Was the information covered in class? What would you do differently next time?

SOME FINAL THOUGHTS

Good assessments are invaluable in helping the classroom teacher determine students' strengths and the strength of the teaching and learning process. Most teachers assess daily through observation, feedback, and paper-and-pencil tests. Great teachers assess their own teaching and how well they are aligning the written, taught, and tested curriculum. If a group of students are not doing well or if the majority of the students are not doing well, great teachers know there is a problem with the alignment system, and they perform an analysis to determine what the problem is. Great teachers know that self-efficacy is important to motivation and strive to assure that all students have an equal and fair chance to be successful. There are no "gotchas" in their assessment processes.

8

State and National Assessments

Tests that have been constructed and field tested so that there is a high degree of reliability and validity are called *standardized tests*. The conditions for taking the tests and for scoring them are uniform and are monitored by the companies or groups that create the tests.

Currently, most state and national standardized tests are either *norm referenced* or *criterion referenced*. A norm-referenced test is one in which student performance is compared to that of a norm group in the content area. The norm group should be composed of students of the same age or grade level as the test takers. Using this type of test allows educators to compare the scores of their students with students in other schools, states, or even classrooms. While individuals are not usually compared against one another, groups of students are compared to determine whether they are making sufficient progress and to make teaching and learning decisions.

A criterion-referenced test compares a student to a given curriculum or level of mastery. States, schools, and classrooms with a predetermined set of criteria or standards for students to know can use a criterion-referenced test to analyze whether students have, in fact, mastered the body of knowledge. The proper use of criterion-referenced tests requires that educators disaggregate the data to determine strengths and weaknesses of individual students and of specific groups (i.e., males, females, socioeconomic groups, minority groups, and by subject area). Many states have moved to using criterion-referenced tests because of their diagnostic, placement, and remediation strengths.

It is interesting to note that the first standardized test in America was given in the mid-1800s in Massachusetts under the direction of Horace Mann, the Secretary of the State Board of Education, in an effort to uniformly classify students and to monitor the effectiveness of the state school system. Proponents of the state testing also hoped to use the test to bring about reform in education. Prior to that time, all assessment was left to the individual classroom teachers.

With the state assessments in Massachusetts, tests became instruments of public policy. It is not surprising that Mann faced some of the same criticism and questions that state and national testing face today. People questioned whether the test measured what the schools were actually teaching and whether the design of the test did what it intended. That debate continues today and, whether we like it or not, testing is here to stay. Governments and other stakeholders want to know if the tax dollars appropriated for education is producing results, and they need some way to measure the results. More and more, funding and other resources are being tied to a school's ability to show results by way of standardized tests.

HOW CAN WE RAISE TEST SCORES NOW?

For those of us in education, there is always a great amount of tension surrounding testing. We teach all learners; that means that we may be teaching students who are reluctant learners or who have come to us working below grade level. We may be dealing with language barriers, cultural barriers, and a lack of sufficient resources to perform the miracles needed to raise test scores immediately. Teachers and administrators scour professional journals and visit workshops hoping for the silver bullet, the one clue that will lead them to helping students experience success. Well, here it is.

THE SILVER BULLET

I want to preface what I am going to say by telling you that I am offering a quick fix for low test scores, a way to provide you some relief so that you can do the long-term things that need to be done to help students over time. *In no way is the information I am providing meant to take the place of in-depth teaching and learning, of providing opportunities for students to develop social skills, or to increase their ability in both declarative and procedural knowledge.* What I am offering is a way to bring up test scores immediately so that all students may experience success. As I have said in all of my books, self-efficacy—the belief one has that one can be successful because one has experienced success in the past—is one of the most powerful ways that we can impact the brain toward motivation.

The silver bullet is divided into two parts.

1. Teach the Vocabulary of the Standardized Test

If you have read my book *What Every Teacher Needs to Know About Instructional Planning* (Tileston, 2004b), you know that teaching vocabulary first in any lesson is critical. According to Sandi Darling (www.learningbridges.com), between 80% and 90% of any standardized test is based on vocabulary (i.e., declarative information). If a student does not understand the vocabulary, we cannot very well expect him or her to be able to understand the information provided, much less use it in some procedural activity. Yet we do this on tests. We give tests based on state and national standards that our students have never seen, heard of, or analyzed for meaning. Let's look at some examples of what I mean.

Example One. This example comes from Texas standards for tenth-grade language arts (available at www.tea.state.tx.us/taks/):

> *Objective 2.* The student will demonstrate an understanding of the effects of literary elements and techniques in culturally diverse written texts.
>   (11) Reading/literary concepts. The student analyzes literary elements for their contributions to meaning in literary tests. The student is expected to (A) compare and contrast varying aspects of texts such as themes, conflicts, and allusions.

As a classroom teacher, I would directly teach the following vocabulary (i.e., declarative knowledge): *analysis, compare and contrast, theme, conflict,* and *allusion.* I would also teach my students the process (i.e., procedural knowledge) of comparing and contrasting by using graphic (i.e., concrete) models so that they could actually create a simple model to help them with the test question. If you are unfamiliar with how to teach students to use compare-and-contrast models, you can find this information in *What Every Teacher Should Know About Effective Teaching Strategies* (Tileston, 2004a) and *What Every Teacher Should Know About Instructional Planning* (Tileston, 2004b).

Example Two. Next, let's look at an elementary example in mathematics. This example is from Grade Four mathematics in Texas.

> *Objective 4.* The student will demonstrate an understanding of the concepts and uses of measurement.
>   (3.11) Measurement. The student selects and uses appropriate units and procedures to measure length and area. The student is expected to (A) estimate and measure lengths using standard units such as inch, foot, yard, centimeter, decimeter, and meter.

Again, as the classroom teacher, I would teach the following vocabulary: *estimate, measure, inch, foot, yard, centimeter, decimeter,* and *meter.* I would teach the process of decision making for measurements. I would use graphic models to help my students remember, because I know that graphic models have a strong influence on our ability to recall information.

2. Use Context for Teaching

Since 80% to 90% of most standardized tests rely on declarative information, such as vocabulary, we must find ways to help students recall declarative information at a more proficient rate. If you have read my book *What Every Teacher Should Know About Learning, Memory, and the Brain* (Tileston, 2004c), you know that declarative information is the most difficult learning for the brain to process and to recall. It is stored in the semantic memory, which is not very good at remembering facts, dates, and vocabulary unless that information is connected to previous information or unless it is connected to one of the other memory pathways. That is one of the reasons students have so much trouble remembering all those facts that we teach them. We can improve our students' ability to recall facts by connecting facts to previous knowledge or experience, paying attention to the test-taking context, and using the other retrieval systems.

Previous knowledge or experience. The brain is a seeker of connections. Anytime that we throw out new information, the brain goes through a moment of chaos while it looks for information or experiences already embedded to which to attach the new information. We can help students facilitate this process by always beginning a new lesson by helping them make connections between old learning and new learning.

Since I have gone through this process at length in other books in this series, I will not go into an in-depth discussion here. However, I will briefly remind you that we can help students make connections by reminding them of previous learning, connecting the new learning to experiences that we know our students have had, or by creating the experience for our students.

For example, if I am teaching a lesson on immigration, I do not assume that my students will know or understand why anyone would get into an inner tube or be stuffed into the cab of a trailer to risk death to come to this country. In order to create a connection to help my students remember the learning, I might ask them what would have to happen in this country to *cause* them to take whatever they could carry in their arms and go to a new country. I might then ask what would have to happen in this country politically—or medically or on the religious front—to make them leave. In asking these questions, I am building a personal connection to the new learning on immigration by building empathy for why people leave their native countries and why they often risk their lives to go to another country.

The test-taking context. Jensen (1997) relates the test results of groups, from elementary age through adulthood, who have taken standardized tests in various locations. The results of the research are pretty overwhelming. If we test people in the same place where they learned the information, they do better on the test. This is related to the pathway of the brain that recalls information based on context—that is, where and how we learned the information. We all tend to do better math in the math classroom than in the English classroom. This is not a fluke; the difference in recall is related to the memory system dependent on context. Rather than moving students to the cafeteria to take a standardized test, try leaving them in their classrooms with their classroom teachers. My belief, based on the research that I have seen, is that your test scores will come up.

Use other retrieval systems. Rather than relying on the semantic memory system for our factual information, we can help our students store and retrieve declarative information more efficiently if we teach with methods that place the factual information into one or more of the other retrieval systems (Tileston, 2000).

In the paragraph above, I discussed the fact that using the other memory systems in conjunction with the semantic memory strengthens students' ability to recall declarative information. A powerful way to accomplish this is through the *episodic memory system,* which, when combined with emotion, can make memories that are recalled for a lifetime. It is the episodic memory system that allows people from my generation to remember where they were when they heard that President Kennedy or Dr. King had been shot even though those events took place many years ago. It is also this memory system that will allow today's generation to remember where they were on September 11, 2001, many years from now.

The *procedural memory system* remembers those things that we "do" with the learning. By combining facts with actions, we help students remember. Graphic models are a great way to help students remember facts, because they combine the process of making the model with the factual information. Movement in the classroom will also tap into this memory system.

In conclusion, once schools begin to use these simple processes, I am convinced that scores will come up significantly. Once students begin to experience success on state and national exams, self-efficacy will be enforced. And once we take some of the pressure off of educators to raise test scores, teachers can begin to make a long-term significant difference in all students' lives.

Vocabulary Summary

Achievement Gap

An *achievement gap* is defined as persistent differences in achievement among different types of students as indicated by scores on standardized tests, teacher grades, and other data. The gaps most frequently referred to are those *between whites and minority* groups, especially African Americans and Hispanics. Another gap of note is *between poor and middle class students*. Over the last decade, that gap has widened so much that some researchers say we now have two classes of students—the haves and the have-nots.

Accountability

In education, *accountability* is currently used to describe the measurable proof that teachers, schools, districts, and states are teaching students efficiently and well. Accountability is usually demonstrated in the form of student success rates on tests.

In recent years, most accountability programs have involved adoption of state curriculum standards and required state tests based on standards. Many political leaders and educators support this approach, believing that it brings clarity of focus and is improving achievement. Others argue that, because standardized tests cannot possibly measure all of the important goals of schooling, accountability systems should be more flexible and use other types of information, such as dropout rates and samples of student work.

Alignment

Alignment refers to the effort to ensure that what teachers teach is in accord with both what the curriculum says will be taught and what is assessed on official tests. When students are not taught the intended content or are not tested on what they were taught, we can expect lower scores. Those lower scores are not an indication of failure on the part of students but rather of a failure on the part of the system. For this reason, schools and school districts often devote considerable attention to alignment. In general, this is a desirable practice. However, alignment can be destructive if the process is driven by tests that themselves are inadequate and if educators feel obligated to teach only what the tests measure.

Aptitude Tests

Aptitude tests attempt to predict a person's ability to do something. The most familiar are intelligence tests, which are intended to measure a person's intellectual abilities. The theory underlying intelligence tests in that each person's mental ability is relatively stable and can be determined apart from his or her knowledge of subject matter or other abilities, such as creativity. Some aptitude tests measure a person's natural ability to learn particular subjects and skills or assess an individual's suitability for certain careers.

Assessment

Assessment is the measurement applied to the learning of information (declarative knowledge) and performance skills (procedural knowledge) on the part of students or teachers. Different types of assessment instruments include achievement tests, minimum competency tests, developmental screening tests, aptitude tests, observation instruments, performance tasks, and authentic assessments.

The effectiveness of a particular approach to assessment depends on its suitability for the intended purpose. For instance, multiple-choice, true/false, and fill-in-the-blank tests can be used to assess basic skills or to find out what students remember. To assess other abilities, performance tasks may be more appropriate.

Performance assessments require students to perform a task, such as serving a volleyball, solving a particular type of mathematics problem, or writing a short story. Sometimes, the task may be designed to assess the student's ability to apply declarative knowledge to procedures or processes. For example, a student might be asked to demonstrate one way that slope is used in the real world.

At-Risk Students

At-risk students are those students who have a higher than average probability of dropping out or failing school. Broad categories of at-risk students usually include inner-city, low-income, and homeless children; those not fluent in English; and special needs students with emotional or behavioral difficulties. Substance abuse, juvenile crime, unemployment, poverty, and lack of adult support are thought to increase a youth's risk factor.

Authentic Assessment

Authentic assessment realistically measures the knowledge and skills needed for success in adult life. The term is often used as an equivalent for *performance assessment*, which, rather than asking students to choose a response to a multiple-choice test item, involves having students perform a task, such as making a basket in basketball, writing a short story, or solving an equation.

Specifically, authentic assessments are not artificial or contrived forms of performance assessments. Most school tests are necessarily contrived: Writing a letter to an imaginary company only to demonstrate to the teacher that you know how to do so is different from writing a letter to a real person or company in order to achieve a real goal. One way to make an assessment more authentic is to have students choose the particular task they will use to demonstrate what they have learned. For example, a student might choose to demonstrate her understanding of a unit in chemistry by developing a model that illustrates the problems associated with oil spills.

Benchmark

A *benchmark* is a standard for judging a performance. Just as an athlete sets benchmarks in time to be able to accomplish certain athletic skills, so students should be given benchmarks by which they can self-evaluate to see if they are making adequate progress. Many state standards also include benchmarks for given grade levels. For example, a broad goal might be that students understand geometric terms. The benchmark at Grade 1 might be that by this grade level students will know basic shapes, such as square, rectangle, and circle. Some schools develop their own benchmarks to tell what students should know by a particular stage of their schooling; for example, "by the end of sixth grade, students should be able to locate major cities and other geographical features on each of the continents."

The classroom teacher sets benchmarks so that he or she will know that students are making adequate progress toward the ultimate goals of the class. This is in contrast to the teacher who covers the subject only to find on the one big assessment at the end that the students did not learn the material. By then, it may be too late to go back and re-teach the lessons.

Competency Tests

Competency tests are created by a school district or state, and students must pass them before graduating. Sometimes called *minimum competency tests,* such tests are intended to ensure that graduates have reached minimal proficiency in basic skills. In recent years, some states have replaced minimum competency tests adopted in the 1970s or 1980s with more demanding tests aligned with adopted curriculum standards.

Criterion-Referenced Tests

Criterion-referenced tests are designed to measure how thoroughly a student has learned a particular body of knowledge without regard to how well other students have learned it. Most nationally standardized achievement tests are norm-referenced, meaning that a student's performance is compared to how well students in a norming group did. Criterion-referenced tests are directly related to the curriculum of a particular school district or state and are scored according to fixed criteria.

Data-Based Decision Making

Data-based decision making is the process of analyzing existing sources of information (e.g., class and school attendance, grades, test scores) and other data (e.g., portfolios, surveys, interviews) to make decisions about a school. The process involves organizing and interpreting the data and creating action plans.

The classroom teacher should make teaching and learning decisions based on available data about the students within the class. This information is used to place students into appropriate instructional groups, determine what strategies are to be used, and how those strategies are to be modified for diverse learners. Even the pacing of the lesson should be driven by data rather than by what "I think and I feel."

Disaggregated Data

Test scores or other data that has been divided so that various categories can be compared is known as *disaggregated data*. For example, schools may break down the data for the entire student population (aggregated into a single set of numbers) to determine how minority students are doing compared with the majority, or how scores of girls compare with those for boys.

Formal Assessments

A *formal assessment* is one to which a grade or judgment is affixed. This is a contrast to an informal assessment, in which the teacher gathers information to help make such decisions about the learning as the appropriate pace to use, what the learners already know, and how the learners perceive the learning. All of the information gathered in informal ways affects the goals and outcomes of the classroom but is not assigned a grade.

Formative Assessments

Formative assessments are tests given primarily to determine what students have learned in order to plan further instruction. In contrast, an examination used primarily to document student's achievement at the end of a unit or course is considered a *summative* test.

High-Stakes Testing

High-stakes tests are used to determine which individual students get rewards, honors, or sanctions. *Low-stakes tests* are used primarily to improve student learning. Tests with high stakes attached include college entrance examinations and exams that students must pass to be promoted to the next grade. Tests affecting the status of schools, such as those on which a given percentage of students must receive a passing grade, are also considered high stakes.

Intelligence Testing

Intelligence tests are used to calculate an individual's intelligence quotient (IQ). IQ is the number derived by dividing a child's "mental age" (derived from his or her score on an intelligence test) by the child's actual age. IQ is based on the principle that children who score well on intelligence tests have a mental ability comparable to older children who are only average. A child whose performance would be expected for his age has an IQ of 100. A child with mental ability considerably higher than his actual age might have an IQ of 130. The term *IQ* is no longer used as frequently as it once was, but intelligence tests continue to be scored using the familiar scale.

Intelligence tests are often used to identify students for special programs, such as gifted and talented programs of special education. Certain cut-off scores are predetermined to indicate gifted, learning disabled, mild mental retardation, and so forth. For example, a school may determine that an IQ score of 130 qualifies a student to be tested further for the gifted program. It should be noted here that no single measure should be used for any special program entry.

Measures of Central Tendency

Measures of central tendency are made up of three dimensions that provide a way to describe the score of a "typical" or "average" student. *Mean* is the arithmetic average score, and it is determined by adding up all the scores and dividing this sum by the total number of scores. The *median* is the midpoint in a distribution of scores from highest to lowest. The *mode* is the score in a distribution that appears most frequently. In a distribution of 95, 90, 88, 86, and 86, the mean is 89, the median is 88, and the mode is 86.

The mean is usually the best indicator of the average; however, when there are a few scores that are either very high or very low compared to the rest of the scores, the median is a better choice to use for the average. The mode is not used as often as the mean or median, but it is appropriate when a large number of the scores are the same.

Although measures of central tendency are important for summarizing sets of student scores, their usefulness often hinges on how widely spread out the scores are. Two sets of scores may have the same mean, but one set of scores may be extremely consistent, with scores clustered close together, while the other set of scores may be very erratic, with a lot of spread between individual scores. *Measures of variability* are used to describe the amount of spread. Two important measures of variability are the *range* and the *standard deviation*. The range is the simplest measure of variability. It is the largest score minus the smallest score in a set of scores. In the set of scores given above, the range is 95–86, or 9 points.

The range gives some indication of the spread of the scores, but its value is determined by only two scores. A measure of variability that takes into account all the scores is the standard deviation. The standard deviation tells how widely spread out the scores are around the mean. If there is no variability in a set of scores, each score would be the same as the mean, giving a standard deviation of zero; the more the scores vary from the mean, the larger the standard deviation. The standard deviation is used extensively in education, particularly with the normal curve and standardized tests.

Natural Distribution

Natural distribution is represented by a bell-shaped curve that describes the distribution of many natural phenomena. Within a natural distribution, approximately 95% of the scores will fall within two standard deviations of the mean, roughly 65% of the scores will fall within one standard deviation above or below the mean, and almost 100% of the scores will fall within three deviations of the mean.

In 1733, Abraham de Moivre (1667–1754) founded the concept of normal distribution. Its implications for statisticians were articulated by mathematician Friedrich Gauss (1777–1855). Thus the normal distribution is sometimes referred to in literature as the *Gaussian distribution*. The bell curve has been used historically to plot physical and psychological information that can be arranged in order of magnitude.

In my book *Ten Best Teaching Practices* (Tileston, 2000), I say that a bell curve is what we might expect at the beginning of a course, but if we continue to get a bell curve after teaching, something is wrong. If we are teaching the material in brain-compatible formats, we should be getting a *J* curve, where most of the students are doing very well. If we are still getting a bell curve, the question we should ask is, "Why aren't my students learning?"

Norm-Referenced Tests

Norm-referenced tests are designed to measure how a student's performance compares with that of other students. Most standardized achievement tests are norm referenced, meaning that a student's performance is compared to the performances of students in a norming group. Scores on norm-referenced tests are often reported in terms of grade-level equivalencies or percentiles derived from the scores of the original students.

Using a norm-referenced test forces a tested group into a bell-shaped curve distribution, whereas a *criterion-referenced test* does not. In a criterion-referenced test, all students could do well or any percentage could do well, since students are not competing against each other.

Peer Assessment

Peer assessment is an assessment that comes from other students. It is done informally—often in the classroom, since students naturally look at each other's work. A formal peer-assessment will have given criteria for scoring another student's work.

Performance Tasks

Performance tasks are activities, exercises, or problems that require students to show what they can do. Some performance tasks are intended to assess a skill, such as solving a particular type of mathematics problem. Others are designed to have students demonstrate their understanding by applying knowledge. To be more authentic (i.e., more like what someone might be expected to do in the adult world), the task and the product from the task might mirror real-world tasks and products.

Performance tasks often have more than one acceptable solution. They may call for a student to create a response to a problem and then explain or defend it. Performance tasks are considered a type of assessment (used instead of, or in addition to, conventional tests), but they may also be used as learning activities.

Portfolio

A collection of student work chosen to exemplify and document a student's learning progress over time is called a *portfolio*. Just as professional artists assemble portfolios of their work, students are often encouraged or required to maintain a portfolio illustrating various aspects of their learning. Some teachers specify what items students should include, while others let students decide. Portfolios are difficult to score reliably and may be a logistical problem for teachers, but advocates say they encourage student reflection and are a more descriptive and accurate indicator of student learning than grades or changes in test scores. Whether portfolios are successful or not seems to depend on the quality of the feedback from the teacher.

Reliability

Reliability is a term used in testing and indicates an estimate of how closely the results of a test would match if that test were given repeatedly to the same student under the same conditions (and if there were no practice effect).

Rubric

A *rubric* contains specific descriptions of different performance levels for a given task. Teachers use rubrics to evaluate student performance on performance tasks. Students are often given the rubric, or may even help develop it, so they know in advance what they are expected to do. For example, the content of an oral presentation might be evaluated using the following rubric:

- Level 4: The main idea is well developed, using important details and anecdotes. The information is accurate and impressive. The topic is thoroughly developed within time constraints.
- Level 3: The main idea is reasonably clear, and supporting details are adequate and relevant. The information is accurate. The topic is adequately developed within time constraints but is not complete.
- Level 2: The main idea is not clearly indicated. Some information is inaccurate. The topic is supported with few details and is sketchy and incomplete.
- Level 1: A main idea is not evident. The information has many inaccuracies. The topic is not supported with details.

Self-Assessment

Self-assessment is an assessment that comes directly from the student. It is the most underused form of classroom assessment but has the most flexibility and power as a combined assessment and learning tool.

Standardized Tests

Standardized tests are administered and scored under uniform (i.e., standardized) conditions. Because most machine-scored, multiple-choice tests are standardized, the term is sometimes used to refer to such tests, but other tests may also be standardized.

Standards

In current usage, the term *standards* usually refers to specific criteria governing what students are expected to learn and be able to do. These standards usually take two forms in the curriculum:

- Content standards (similar to what were formerly called *goals* and *objectives*), which tell what students are expected to know and be able to do in various subject areas, such as mathematics and science.
- Performance standards, which specify what levels of learning are expected. Performance standards assess the degree to which content standards have been met.

In recent years, standards have also been developed specifying what teachers should know and be able to do.

Student Understanding

Student understanding cannot be measured easily by forced-choice type questions. Students who understand can interpret, can explain, can empathize, and can use the information in meaningful ways.

Summative Assessment

Summative assessment is a test given to evaluate and document what students have learned. Summative assessment tests are different from formative tests, which are used primarily to diagnose what students have learned in order to plan further instruction.

Validity

In testing, *validity* indicates how well a test measures what it is intended to measure. For example, a test in history may be so difficult for young students to read that it is more of a reading test than a test of historical knowledge. That makes it invalid for its intended purpose.

Vocabulary
Post-Test

At the beginning of this book, you were given a vocabulary list and a pre-test on that vocabulary. Below is the post-test. How would you answer the questions now? The answer key for the vocabulary assessment is also given below.

VOCABULARY POST-TEST

Instructions: Choose the one best answer for the questions given.

1. Mr. Conner wants to know if his students can apply the information they learned on estimation. Which assessment would be the best way to determine whether the students can apply what they know?
   A. Multiple-choice test
   B. Forced-choice test
   C. Self-assessment
   D. Performance task

2. A test that determines whether a student graduates from high school is . . .
   A. Criterion referenced
   B. High stakes
   C. Norm referenced
   D. A performance task

3. In a normal distribution, what percentage of the scores falls within two standard deviations of the mean?
   A. 95%
   B. 90%
   C. 85%
   D. 97%

4. The XYZ Testing Company is retesting a group of students to see how closely the test scores match the first test given. For what are they testing?
   A. Validity
   B. Performance
   C. Reliability
   D. Bias

5. Using measures of central tendency, when would it be appropriate to use the mode?
   A. When the standard deviation is zero.
   B. When the scores are average.
   C. When a large number of the scores are the same.
   D. When there is a large distribution in the scores.

6. Which term reflects the spread of scores around the mean?
   A. Standard deviation
   B. Median
   C. Mode
   D. Validity

7. A test given to determine what students have learned in order to plan instruction is . . .
   A. A norm-referenced test
   B. Formative assessment
   C. A forced-choice test
   D. An aptitude test

8. A test given to document what a student has learned is called . . .
   A. Summative assessment
   B. An aptitude test

C. A criterion-referenced test

D. Formative assessment

9. Martin School makes a strong effort to ensure that what is written in their curriculum documents is what is taught in the classroom and what is tested. This practice is know as . . .

A. Competency

B. Data-based decision making

C. Benchmarks

D. Alignment

10. Martin School regularly looks at test scores to determine if male students are performing as well as female students and to see that minorities are making the same level of progress as majority students. This practice is called . . .

A. Prevention of bias

B. Disaggregating data

C. Setting benchmarks

D. Authentic assessment

11. The teachers at Martin School have taken the information from test scores, as well as attendance and dropout rates, to plan for student needs. This practice is called . . .

A. Benchmarking

B. Disaggregating data

C. Data-based decision making

D. Using reliability

12. Martin School is examining student test scores, particularly to compare male and female scores and the scores of students by race. For what are they most likely looking?

A. Validity

B. Achievement gaps

C. Reliability

D. Norms

13. To measure students' progress over time on performance tasks, which type of assessment would most likely be used?
    A. Portfolios
    B. Forced-choice tests
    C. Achievement tests
    D. Norm-referenced tests

14. To test declarative knowledge, a teacher would probably use which type of assessment?
    A. Forced-choice tests
    B. Portfolios
    C. Performance tasks
    D. Observation

15. To test procedural knowledge, a teacher would probably use which type of assessment?
    A. Multiple-choice tests
    B. Essay
    C. True/false tests
    D. Observation

16. Mr. Conner's school resides in a state that has adopted state curriculum standards for which students are tested annually. This practice is often referred to as . . .
    A. Assessment
    B. Authentic assessment
    C. Alignment
    D. Accountability

17. On the XYZ test, about 20% of the students failed, about 20% did very well, and the rest of the students scored in between. This is called . . .
    A. Reliability
    B. Validity
    C. Normal distribution
    D. Standardization

18. The measure that is applied to learning is called . . .
    A. Reliability
    B. Assessment
    C. Evaluation
    D. Validity

19. Which type of test most closely assesses how well students know state standards?
    A. Criterion-referenced tests
    B. Aptitude tests
    C. Formative assessments
    D. Norm-referenced tests

20. Which of the following is *not* true of state testing?
    A. They are formative in nature.
    B. They are summative in nature.
    C. They are based on content standards.
    D. They are based on performance standards.

Post-Test Answer Key

1. D		11. C	
2. B		12. B	
3. A		13. A	
4. C		14. A	
5. D		15. D	
6. A		16. D	
7. B		17. C	
8. A		18. B	
9. D		19. A	
10. B		20. A	

References

Gardner, H. (1983). *Frames of mind: The theory of multiple intelligences.* New York: Basic Books.

Jensen, E. (1997). *Completing the puzzle: The brain-compatible approach to learning* (2nd ed.). Del Mar, California: Turning Point.

Jensen, E. (1998). *Introduction to brain-compatible learning.* Del Mar, CA: Turning Point.

Marzano, R. J. (1998). *A theory-based meta-analysis of research on instruction.* Aurora, CO: Mid-continent Regional Educational Laboratory.

Marzano, R. J. (2000). *Transforming classroom grading.* Alexandria, VA: Association for Supervision and Curriculum Development.

Piaget, J. (1973). *To understand is to invent.* NY: Viking.

Silver, H. F., Strong, R. W., & Perini, M. J. (2000). *So each may learn.* Alexandria, VA: Association for Supervision and Curriculum Development.

Sprenger, M. (2002). *Becoming a wiz at brain-based teaching: How to make every year your best year.* Thousand Oaks, CA: Corwin.

Stiggins, R. J. (1994). *Student-centered classroom assessment* (2nd ed.). Columbus, OH: Merrill.

Tileston, D. W. (2000). *Ten best teaching practices: How brain research, learning styles, and standards define teaching.* Thousand Oaks, CA: Corwin.

Tileston, D. W. (2004a). *What every teacher should know about effective teaching strategies.* Thousand Oaks, CA: Corwin.

Tileston, D. W. (2004b). *What every teacher should know about learning, memory, and the brain.* Thousand Oaks, CA: Corwin.

Tileston, D. W. (2004c). *What every teacher should know about instructional planning.* Thousand Oaks, CA: Corwin.

Wiggins, G., & McTighe, J. (1998). *Understanding by design.* Alexandria, VA: Association for Supervision and Curriculum Development.

Index

**CORWIN
PRESS**

The Corwin Press logo—a raven striding across an open book—represents the happy union of courage and learning. We are a professional-level publisher of books and journals for K-12 educators, and we are committed to creating and providing resources that embody these qualities. Corwin's motto is "Success for All Learners."